KID CONFIDENCE

A Parent's Guide: How to build resilience
and develop self-esteem in your child

WRITTEN BY
Susan Garcia

Disclaimer Notice:

Please note the information contained within this document is for educational and entertainment purposes only. All effort has been executed to present accurate, up to date, and reliable, complete information. No warranties of any kind are declared or implied. Readers acknowledge that the author is not engaging in the rendering of legal, financial, medical or professional advice. The content within this book has been derived from various sources. Please consult a licensed professional before attempting any techniques outlined in this book.

By reading this document, the reader agrees that under no circumstances is the author responsible for any losses, direct or indirect, which are incurred as a result of the use of information contained within this document, including, but not limited to, — errors, omissions, or inaccuracies

Table of Contents

Introduction

Confidence. When you think about it, you imagine a child who is not afraid to speak their mind, one who can stand in front of others and give their speech without quivering, and one who makes and keeps friends easily. But it doesn't always work like that. Often, the very things we want for our kids seem to elude us.

The lack of confidence can be a result of a lot of things. Sometimes, it's the rivalry between siblings that triggers it, other times a teacher whose too harsh, and sometimes, our parenting style. We can try all we can, but if our kids don't feel loved, their confidence will suffer.

Confidence cannot be given. It's a vague concept that kids find difficult to understand. You can tell your child to be confident in their ability, and even use shapes and diagrams to demonstrate what they should do, but unless our child cultivates this habit, they will continue to be shy and suffer from low self-esteem.

But that doesn't mean there is nothing you can do to help. Far from it. There are steps you can take to help your child cultivate confidence, and this book will outline them for you. We will look at how to spot when your child has no confidence, what to do about sibling rivalry, and how to handle a child who doesn't handle constructive criticism well.

Using real-life examples, we will look at how a child's self-esteem changes throughout their development stages, what to do if your child gives up too easily, and how to help them accept their faults as a learning process. Decisions are not easy for kids, and sometimes they learn to depend on us to help them. Life does not work that way though, and kids need to learn how to make their own decisions. A confident child will make decisions and follow-through. We will show you how to help your child if they depend on you to decide for them.

Chapter One: How Low Self-Esteem Develops

How to understand when your child has low self-esteem

Stacy was excited to take her little boy to daycare. He was an only child and he didn't have a lot of people to play with. But today, he would have a chance to make some new friends. Stacy was excited. If this experience went well, she planned to make this a regular thing. She went to extensive lengths to look for the perfect daycare, where her little boy would not only get the care he needed, but one with tons of toys he would enjoy as well. The kids seemed friendly and their caregivers were professional and seemed happy.

The first few days seemed ok, and Stacy thought everything was going well. She was finally settled and could go back to work in peace. Then she started to notice a few changes. Her son was always excited to come home and he seemed to brighten whenever they were around. When asked about his day, he would respond that it was fine, but he would never get into details of what happened, the friends he made or anything like that.

Stacy did not read much into it. She thought that maybe he needed a little more time to adapt to the new environment. When she went back to work, she forgot about her son's issue for what seemed like a little while. She became engrossed in running her department and integrating back into work that her family had to take a back seat. At least for a while. She would occasionally ask her little boy about his day, but the answer was always the same. "It was ok. I played with my truck."

Things did not change when he went to kindergarten. He seemed excited to join but soon went back to his cocoon. Stacy went to school to ask his teacher about it, but nothing seemed to be a miss per se. He was just one of the "quiet ones". When her son started complaining a lot, something in Stacy told her that maybe there was something wrong. Maybe he needed some help with something. But when the tantrums became apparent, she was forced to be a little tough on him. "You can't have it your way all the time," she would constantly tell him.

One day at dinner, her husband asked a question that made Stacy look at the situation from a different angle. "Who's your friend at school Tom?" Stacy looked at her son, eager to finally hear him talk about his schoolmates. But her little boy took a while to answer, thinking hard. When he finally answered, his eyes never left his food, his voice was low, and his hands fidgety.

"I don't know. I really don't have friends."
"So who do you play with?"

"My toys mostly. Or I draw."

"I'm sure you must have someone you talk to," she prodded.

Pause.

"Not really. I guess they never want to play with me because I don't know the games."

"What if you learned how to play? It would be fun to learn something new, right?" She tried again, looking at her husband to contribute. He watched, probably too stunned to know what to say.

"There is no use. They won't teach me."

Another long pause. Stacy did not know how to respond. She could feel the pain her child was going through, and at this moment, she was helpless. Anything she said after this would probably not help the situation. She looked at her husband pleading with her eyes for help.

"Tell you what buddy, why don't I teach you some games over the weekend?"

"Sure."

Stacy and her husband looked at each other. Their once excited, full of life boy was now timid and shy. She did not understand this. When did this happen? Stacy noticed that Tom had lost weight, and he had barely touched his food that evening. She instantly became worried and lost her own appetite. How was she going to help?

Confidence in kids is the same as confidence in an adult. It's how a person views themselves and what they believe to be true even if it isn't. A child with a healthy view of themselves develops into a healthy confident adult, which is what we all want for our kids. The confidence and self-worth of your child will change at different stages in development, and most parents depend on physical things to notice the change.

You notice their verbal and non-verbal skills, maintaining eye contact, eating habits, among others. Like Stacy's case, monitoring your child's self-esteem is not always a great concern unless you notice something is terribly wrong. Your child will have gone through a lot of wounds, tried to communicate their dissatisfaction in life and their feelings of inadequacy, but somehow, you will miss them.

This is usually because parents don't know what to look out for. When kids are young, it's not easy to notice when their esteem is suffering. It's always more noticeable when they start school because self-confidence becomes more apparent. Noticing a lack of confidence when your child is younger, however, prevents more serious issues when they are older. There are several ways to know if your child is suffering.

Direct manifestation

Shame

With some kids, it's easy to tell when they are weighed down, often in how they talk about themselves. Listen to your child and watch out for words such as "I'm stupid, I can't make any friends, I'll never get it done, I can't do it, there is no point in trying," and tons of other phrases like these ones. Often, your child will be in despair, seem sad, or lose hope. Their faces will be dim, and their shoulders and head will be down.

In Stacy's case, for instance, her son's behavior coupled with how he spoke about having friends was a clear sign that he has low self-esteem. Stacy does not need anyone to spell it out for her. When talking about friends, Tom's shoulders and head were down, he avoided eye contact, and his voice was low and timid. This is a sign of shame. Kids who feel shameful adapt postures that make them feel small, such as shoulders down and low tones.

Pessimism and exaggeration

It's often difficult for your child to enjoy anything else if they don't feel good about themselves. For instance, your child will usually predict a negative outcome to situations when you and others view it very differently. The glass will always be half empty in their eyes. In some cases, kids also tend to exaggerate the situation in a bid to get sympathy and attention from others. It works for a while, but eventually, it fails and only makes them feel worse about themselves.

Blame games

We all want to believe that it's not our fault that we feel how we feel. The same goes for kids. They will either sink into the extreme of blaming themselves and feel helpless, believing that nothing can be done, or blame others. If only this would change them things would get better is the motto they live with. The problem with this is that deep down they know it's not true, and eventually, it leads to shame.

Using coping strategies to mask low self-esteem

Kids like Tom can easily express their low self-esteem, but it's not always the same for all kids. Some kids, especially teens, will mask it by adapting coping mechanisms. It becomes difficult for parents to know something is wrong unless they take a keen, close look at their kids. This is often seen in kids with learning difficulties. The kids believe that their failures and mistakes are out of their control, and they develop what psychologists refer to as "learned helplessness." Their image of the future is filled with failure, and they cannot see light at the end of the tunnel.

Kids and adults naturally develop coping mechanisms to help them manage everyday stress and changes. But there is a significant difference between kids with high self-esteem and those with low esteem. Kids with high self-esteem will develop mechanisms that are adaptive and lead to self-mastery and growth. For instance, they will get a math tutor if they are having a problem in math. A child with low self-esteem will adopt one of these coping mechanisms.

Quitting

Kids can become easily frustrated when they can't succeed at a task, that they quit. Once they quit, they often offer excuses and avoid doing the task altogether. Ever heard your child say "it's dumb or it's boring?" That's a sign of quitting.

Avoiding and clowning

This behavior is a close relative of quitting. The difference is in avoiding, the child does not want to start the task altogether. In quitting, they will have started, and abandon the task in the middle as they fear lurking doom. Kids often start to make jokes and act silly when they feel pressured to do something. This is called clowning.

Controlling

A lot of kids often become controlling and try to tell everyone else what to do as they try to mask their feelings of inadequacy. For example, they will want their classmates to play the games they choose. If they don't comply, the child will abandon the game and refuse to join the others.

Aggressiveness and bullying

When they feel vulnerable, kids tend to bully others to mask their feelings. They spot victims who show certain weaknesses, often the ones they themselves suffer from, and make them feel worse about it.

Impulsiveness and denying

Being impulsive is often a child's temperament, but kids with low self-esteem use it to mask their true feelings. For instance, kids will finish their work quickly, even when it's not well done, so they can get out of a task they don't like. Kids will mask their insecurities by denying they are worried about something.

Praising Your Child and Self-Esteem

For many years, conventional wisdom stated that praising a child at every opportunity boosted their confidence and self-esteem. However, in recent years, new research has shown that the wrong kind of praise and too much praise actually undermine your child's confidence. Even worse, unearned praise or non-specific praise can derail the natural development of perseverance and resilience.

A recent study on how the wrong kind of praise can backfire was conducted at Stanford University. Twenty, fifth-graders were given problems that required some effort but were easy to solve, so most of them got them right. Afterward, half the students were told they were smart and praised for their achievement, and the other half was commended for their efforts. After a little while, the children were given the choice of taking more difficult tests or another test like the first one. The children who were praised for their efforts were eager to take on the harder problems. But the ones honored for their achievements shied away or chose to do similar tests, which they knew they would pass.

The researchers concluded that simply telling the children they were smart, awesome, or geniuses was actually setting them up and keeping them from making mistakes that would undermine their 'smart' image.

Moderating praise is easier said than done. All parents want their kids to know how great they are and that they can do anything they set their minds to. However, there must be a balance between cheering them on and fostering their development. Too much praise can turn a good thing into a bad thing. As a parent, you want to boost your child's confidence without increasing their vanity.

When you tell your kid that you are proud of them, it shouldn't be solely based on their performance. In fact, they are set to learn more from failure than when passing or excelling at things.

When to praise your child

It is essential to know when to deliver praise and when not to and to also understand what form the praise should take. If a kid is praised for doing trivial things and commonplace effort such as "Wow, way to go, buddy, you woke up early this morning!", your praise will lose its power and meaning. Why work for something that you will get regardless of whether you try or not? In this case, your praise simply becomes part of the background noise, something they are used to hearing.

Non-specific praise like saying, "You're awesome!" can also undermine your child's confidence. It is because they have no way of knowing what that really means and what makes them awesome. They have nothing to compare themselves to, and thus lack an understanding of what it takes to achieve this" awesomeness."

Praise as a positive reward and its role

A reward is defined as a prize or other mark of recognition given in honor of an achievement. It is something that is earned after some effort has been put in. A reward is an incentive that increases a target behavior. Studies have shown that if the target behavior was to decrease, what you think is a reward is actually punishment. The "You are smart" and "You are awesome" forms of praise show that even with positive words, the desired outcome, which is more shows of intelligence or good behavior, decreases. In this case, the positive affirmations function as punishment.

A reward that is given too often loses its power and influence to shape behavior. This phenomenon is referred to as satiation. The same thing can happen with praise. It is not unusual for children to tune out approval from a doting parent.

Parental attention and response are an inherent part of intuitive parenting and can serve as powerful rewards in themselves. When your child brings you something she made, don't say how great it looks and tell her she is awesome. Instead, take time to ask her how she made it? What materials did she use? If she had any help and if she is thinking of making something else? Showing genuine interest in her work will encourage her to focus more on the process and not the result. This is called a praise transaction. Everyone, especially kids, loves having someone take an interest in what they are doing and engage with them this way.

Remember, the praise should increase desired behaviors, which in this case is having the child continue being creative and express her creativity positively. What you want in the end, is for the child to gain enough confidence to express herself, continue in her innovative ways, and be resilient enough to tackle any obstacles, challenges, or people with different opinions. It is these behaviors and skills, not the empty praise, that will foster your child's self-esteem as they grow up.

Your attention and interest in what your child is doing can remain as a form of praise, even when they fail or make mistakes. These moments provide valuable teaching opportunities to reward resilience and persistence. By encouraging them and praising their efforts, you are empowering them to try again. The continuous engagement shows your child that failure is not the end, and failing does not make them less smart or less impressive in your eyes.

How to praise effectively

Matthew, a natural athlete, was widely praised from an early age for his throwing and catching abilities by his parents. Once he was old enough to play with other kids, he realized, for the first time, that he was good—but maybe not the best. In Little League games, he would choke up, unable to catch or throw any ball. He also constantly looked back to his parents for encouragement and kept forgetting to keep his eye on the ball. He would get upset if his every effort wasn't met with praise from his coach, even when such accolades wouldn't help him perform any better. Matthew was a bundle of nerves out in the real world, unlike when he played with his dad in the backyard, and he got endless praise.

1. Be sincere about your praise

As you can see, this is a classic case of how praise, the wrong kind of praise, affected a child's ability to play. His parents wanted him to know that he was good at baseball but overdid it, which turned Matthew into someone who needed his every action noticed and praised. This kept him from becoming a good baseball player. His parents should have praised his efforts and accomplishments when he learned to catch or throw the ball right. With this kind of praise, he would have put more effort into practicing, and he would have become better.

2. Praise specifically

Instead of generalizing everything, state what the child did to earn the accolades. It is also important to tell them how you feel about it. For instance, if your son picks up his toys from the floor, say, "I appreciate that you picked up your toys without me having to ask." or "thank you for helping me keep the house looking neat and clean by picking up your toys." Young children do not need praise all the time. The best thing you can do is highlight what you think they did well.

You should also avoid praising your child in areas they do not have control over. This can include innate and unalterable abilities such as intelligence, physical attractiveness, athleticism, or artistic gifts. Instead, you should direct your praise to areas they have control over, such as effort, attitude, responsibility, commitment, discipline, focus, decision making, compassion, generosity, respect, love, etc.

You should also understand that kids are more likely to incorporate the specific praise they hear from their parents into their view of themselves. Matthew knew he was praised for being the best from an early age. So when he interacted with other kids, he quickly realized that even though he was good, he was probably not the best. This affected him as he did not understand why his coach never praised him.

3. Learn when to praise

Praise your child after an accomplishment or a good deed. You don't have to honor your child continually. For instance, if you want your daughter to have completed her homework by a certain time, work out a plan, and make a homework schedule. You can then praise her when homework is indeed done on time.

After the behavior has been learned or changed, you can decrease the frequency of reinforcement. Once the homework schedule becomes routine, you can gradually stop the consistent praise; but you can keep an eye on things and occasionally say something like, "Boy, you remembered to do your homework and on time, even when I didn't remind you." These few words are a type of praise and can be very reassuring to a child. Remember, if you want to foster a particular behavior in your kid, "catch them being good" by recognizing it.

When you comment on and describe clearly a specific behavior that shows their capability, your kids are more likely to adopt that message into their self-view. On a deeper level, they become more aware and accepting of their own strengths and abilities. So the child who picks up his toys may begin to think of himself as a helper or a cooperative family member who can contribute to his home.

By giving your kids distinct positive images of themselves, you are equipping them to deal with some of the challenges they may encounter in the "outside world." Specific, sincere praise is part of conscious parenting. It can be hard work, and it also requires practice, but the pay-off over time is tremendous. Praise can impact how your children feel about themselves. So you want to role out the right kind. As you concentrate on praising your children effectively, keep in mind that each child is unique and may take in your praise in a different way depending on his or her temperament.

How children's self-esteem changes at different ages

Considered one of the most important components of emotional health, self-esteem is a combination of self-confidence and self-acceptance. It's how individuals perceive themselves and their self-value. Self-esteem is the way you think and feel about yourself and how it affects how well you do things that are important to you. In kids, it is shaped by what they think and how they feel about themselves. Their esteem is highest when they see themselves nearing what they perceive as their ideal self or who they would like to be.

Children with high self-esteem have an easier time dealing with conflict, resisting negative pressure and making friends. They are generally happier and have a more optimistic view of life. On the other hand, kids with low self-esteem have a harder time dealing with conflict, they are overly critical of themselves and become passive, withdrawn and sometimes even depressed. They can be hesitant when it comes to trying new things and get easily frustrated. They often see problems as permanent conditions that cannot change and thus have a dull pessimistic outlook on life.

Self-esteem sources

For children, self-esteem can come from different sources at different stages in their development. The development of a child's self-esteem is highly influenced by the parents' attitudes and behaviors. In the early childhood stages, a number of factors play a role in developing self-esteem. For instance, supportive parental behavior such as encouragement and praise as well as the child's internalization of his parents' attitudes toward success or failure, are the two most powerful influences in the development of self-esteem. As they grow older, other influences such as their experiences in school, with their peers and outside the home environment, play an increasingly important role in determining their levels of self-esteem.

On average self-esteem is relatively high during early childhood and drops during adolescence especially in girls, rises gradually through adulthood, then drops again during old age. Young children have relatively high self-esteem, which gradually declines as they grow up. Researchers speculate that children have a high sense of self-esteem because their self-views are unrealistically positive.

As children develop cognitively, they begin to base their self-evaluations on external feedback and social comparisons and thus form a more balanced and accurate appraisal of their academic competence, social skills, attractiveness, and other personal characteristics. For example, as they move from preschool to elementary school they can receive more negative feedback from teachers, parents, and peers. This can affect their self-evaluations making them become more negative. There is a continuous drop in self-esteem throughout adolescent due to the changes that occur during puberty.

Schools can influence your child's self-esteem through the attitudes they promote toward competition and diversity and their recognition of academic, sports and artistic achievements. By middle childhood, friendships assume a pivotal role in your child's life. Studies have shown that school-age children spend more time with their friends than watching tv, playing alone or doing homework. Also, the amount of time they interact with their parents is greatly reduced compared to when they were younger. At this stage, social acceptance by a child's peer group plays a major role in developing and maintaining self-esteem.

The physical and emotional developments that happen during adolescence, especially in the early stages, present new trials to your child's self-esteem. Boys who are late bloomers often compare themselves with their peers who matured early and appear more athletic, masculine, and confident. In contrast, maturing early can be embarrassing for girls. Many feel awkward and self-conscious in their newly developed bodies. Both boys and girls spend a lot of time on personal grooming.

They also spend long periods in the bathroom trying to achieve a particular look. It becomes essential for them and their self-esteem that they fit in with their peers. In later adolescence, their associations with the opposite sex (or sometimes the same sex) can become a significant source of confidence or insecurity. It is, therefore, important for adolescents to gain a sense of competence by making and learning from their mistakes. By being held accountable for their actions, they learn what they are capable of and that all actions have consequences.

Peer acceptance and relationships are vital to children's social and emotional development and their self-esteem. Being accepted by their peers, especially in friendships, provides a broad scope of learning and development opportunities for children. These include friendship, entertainment, social skills, participating in group problem solving, and managing competition and conflict. They also support self-exploration, emotional development, and moral and ethical growth.

Factors that influence self-esteem

Several factors influence self-esteem. These include:

1. Age

Self-esteem in children tends to grow steadily until middle school. The transition of moving from the everyday environment of elementary school to a new setting confronts children with new demands. Their self-esteem either continues to grow or begins to decrease.

2. Gender

Girls tend to be more susceptible to getting low self-esteem than boys. This could be due to the increased social pressure that stresses appearance more than intelligence or athletic capability.

3. Socioeconomic status

According to research, children from higher-income families have a better sense of self-esteem in their mid- to late-adolescence years. The socioeconomic class of a child and their family can affect how they feel and the views they have of themselves.

4. Body image

This is especially true for teenagers, but it also applies to younger children. A child creates their body image from what they see on tv, movies, adverts, and social media. Girls are often portrayed as having a certain body type with perfect complexion and hair. The boys, on the other hand, are described as muscular, very handsome, and tall. Girls and boys who do not fit in the portrayed image often have low self-esteem because they are comparing themselves with these cultural and narrow standards.

Self-esteem at different childhood stages

1. Infancy

Infants start developing self-esteem as soon as they are born. Their self-esteem is first increased by having their basic needs met, which include the need for love, comfort, and closeness. They gradually realize that they are loved as the people who care for them always treat them kindly, comfort them when they cry, and show them attention. How their parents or primary caregivers treat them at this stage sets precedence for later self-esteem development. Parents who shower their babies with love and attention teach the infants that they are valued, safe, and secure.

2. Toddlerhood

Toddlers still have not developed a clear sense of self-esteem or self-identity. Every time they learn a new skill, they add to their abilities and their comprehension of who they are. Toddlers learn more about themselves by learning what they look like, what they can do, and where they belong. It can be difficult for them to share things as they are now discovering who they are and what is theirs.

Toddlers perceive themselves through the eyes of their parents, family, or primary caregivers. If their parents show them love and tell them that they are special, they will develop a strong sense of self-esteem. Toddlers who feel unloved or not as special to their parents find it more difficult to develop a sense of self-worth.

3. Preschooler

By the time they turn three, kids have a clearer understanding of who they are and how they fit into the world as they know it. They are now more self-aware and have begun learning about their bodies. They also find that they can think and make decisions on their own to some limits. They can handle being away from their parents for some time because they feel loved and safe when among others. Their self-esteem develops mostly in physical ways, such as comparing their appearance to that of other children either by height, size, and abilities.

Preschoolers acquire self-esteem in stages through growing their senses of trust, independence, and drive. At this age, parents can help to foster self-esteem in their kids by teaching them problem-solving skills, involving them in tasks that give them a sense of accomplishment, asking for and listening to their views, and presenting them in social settings, notably with their peers. These young children get self-esteem through what they can do and by valuing what their parents think of them.

4. School-age children

A decisive point in a child's self-esteem development occurs when they start school. For many, their self-esteem falls when they have to cope with adults and peers in a new setting with rules that are new and strange. In the beginning, self-esteem is about how well the children succeed in learning tasks in school and how they performed in sports. Their physical appearance, characteristics, and their ability to make friends with other children their age also plays a part in the development of self-esteem.

5. Teenagers

Teenagers' self-esteem is often affected by the physical and hormonal changes they encounter. This is especially true during puberty. They undergo major body changes, which can affect their self-esteem, making it fragile. Teenagers are extremely concerned about their looks and how they are regarded and accepted by their peers. Teens who have set goals for themselves have more self-esteem than those who do not. High self-esteem is also directly related to having a very supportive family.

Body image is a major part of teenagers' self-esteem development. They care what their peers will say about them and how they will see them. Teens with high self-esteem are confident in their looks and accept themselves the way they are. For teenagers with low self-esteem, they often have a poor body image and are often too critical of themselves. They might think they are too fat, not pretty enough, or not muscular enough.

They must learn that there are some physical features that they cannot change, such as being tall or short. But by accepting themselves as they are, without undue self-criticism, they can boost their self-esteem levels. If there are things that cause low self-esteem but can be altered, teens may be able to set reasonable goals to help them make the change. For instance, if your teenage daughter thinks she is overweight, before slumming and giving up to a negative mindset, she should confirm this with a health care provider. If they confirm that she is actually overweight, help her set weight loss goals such as eating nutritiously and exercising frequently.

For teens with low-self esteem, they need to know that they can stop these bad thoughts and instead focus on boosting their sense of self-worth. You can encourage them to try doing positive thinking exercises, such as complimenting yourself daily. By focusing on the good things they do and the positive aspects of their lives, they can change how they feel about themselves. Parents can improve teenagers' self-esteem by asking for their help or advice and welcoming their opinions.

A lot of things can hurt a child's sense of self-worth. Stressors at home, such as parents who argue a lot, and problems at school, like difficult lessons, bullies, or being unable to make friends. Children with overly developed self-esteem can be bullies to those with low self-esteem. Parents can assist their children in developing an inner sense of self-control, which comes from having experience in making decisions.

Common problems that cause self-esteem issues

Many studies have associated low self-esteem to a wide range of problems, such as poor school performance, criminal and violent tendencies; being the victim of bullying; teenage pregnancy; smoking and taking alcohol as well as other drugs; dropping out of school; depression; suicidal thoughts, suicide attempts, and they can even end up committing suicide.

Also, children and teens who have low self-esteem have more physical health problems than those with higher self-esteem.

Parental concerns

Every child and teen has had low self-esteem at some point in his or her life. Criticism from parents or others can make children with low self-esteem feel even worse. Children can also exhibit low self-esteem if their parents or others press them to attain unrealistic goals. Parents should be concerned when a child's low self-esteem affects his or her daily activities or leads to depression. Some common signs of low-self-esteem in children and teens are as follows:

- The need to always please others.
- General feelings of dislike towards themselves.
- Feeling unhappy most of the time.
- They see their problems as abnormal and that they are to blame.
- They needing constant validation or approval for everything they do.
- They cannot make friends easily or having no friends at all.
- They have a constant need to prove that they are better than others at anything they do.

When to seek professional help

Sometimes a lack of self-esteem is too much for a child to handle alone. Parents may need to seek professional psychological help when the child is depressed or shows an inability to make friends. Help may also be required for adolescents whose lack of self-esteem is expressed in negative behaviors, such as engaging in criminal activities, gang affiliation, smoking, and alcohol and other drug dependencies. If the child talks about or threatens to commit suicide, professional help should be sought immediately.

Chapter Two: Connection

What to do when your child reacts badly to your correction

Children respond differently to correction, and while the cause could be various things, how your child responds says a lot about them and their level of confidence. Some kids don't respond to punishment or discipline. They put on what parents call a stubborn face, and it's common for parents to refer to them as bad or stubborn kids. They react to time outs with defiance and shrug off any consequence to their actions.

It can be quite frustrating for parents, and this behavior becomes a ticking time bomb. Parents feel like they can blow up at any moment. Dad's are especially not nice when this happens. Unlike moms, dads tend to see a child who doesn't listen as one who does not respect them. Although sometimes it's a stage that every child must go through, it's nerve-wracking when the video games, music, or toy becomes more important than you.

Whether you are raising a strong-willed child or an energetic one, there are common bad reactions to correction that arise in most kids you should note.

1. Lying

   Kids have three main reasons why they lie. First, they want to get your attention. This happens to kids who feel that there is little positive attention to go round. Second, to avoid getting into trouble. Most kids know when they do something wrong, and because they don't want to face the consequences of their actions, they lie. Lastly, to feel good about themselves. Everyone, including kids, wants to feel that they have some power over their life. If they feel helpless and that they lack control, they will look for other avenues to get back this control. Lying is one of these avenues.

2. Defiance

   Have you ever asked your child to do something, and they openly ignored you? Defiance is one of the toughest behaviors to deal with. It's usually met with threats when you can't take it any longer. "If you don't do X, then you don't get Y later" is a common phrase parents use. Kids are usually defiant because of a few reasons. First, they are testing your limits to see how far they can go with something or what the consequence is. Secondly, because they seek negative attention. This could be because they feel they are not getting enough attention, or for the fun of it.

Sometimes, your child is too engrossed in an activity that they hear you talk, but they don't really hear you. Defiant kids are also rejecting their parents as leaders, an indication that they feel disconnected from the parent. The punishment parents dish out only makes the child more rebellious and the disconnection worse.

3. A disrespectful child

Teens are fond of rolling their eyes when they are disrespectful, while preteens will say things like "whatever dad" when you tell them to do something like start their homework or clean their room. Although not always, refusing to turn off electronics can be considered a mild disrespect. Serious disrespect includes name-calling, throwing things around, shouting, physical aggression, and disregarding rules.

Disrespectful kids are usually in a power struggle with their parents. They feel controlled and are looking for a way to exert themselves. It could also be a sign that they need to learn how to deal with frustrations, manage anger, and learn effective communication. Such kids need to learn social skills, or they will be the ones hitting other kids at the playground and school. If disrespect is not corrected, kids grow up to be rude adults that no one wants to associate with.

40

4. Whining

Kids who whine are not necessarily spoilt or annoyed. Instead, they complain because they want our attention or to get something. Whining works and kids know it! They know it's irritating and that they will get whatever they want if they whine. It's likely to happen when kids are bored, tired, sick, hungry, and when they want attention. It's mostly common in kids between three and six years. But how long it continues will depend on how much and how often you cave in when your child whines.

5. Aggression

Aggression comes in many ways, including your child throwing their book when homework becomes frustrating and hitting their sister when they are mad. Sometimes kids are aggressive because they can't handle their own feelings while other times it's merely because they know it will catch your attention.

What to do when your correction are no longer effective?

When Mary's second daughter was born, she was confident of her disciplining techniques that worked incredibly well with her firstborn. Two years down the line, my sweet innocent baby made me doubt everything I know. You see, her firstborn was petrified of being spanked and she always straightens up before Mary got there. This little one, however, was not afraid of anything. Shout, yell, timeouts didn't scare her at all. In fact, she challenged Mary to dish out the punishment and get it over with so she can go back to whatever she was doing.

Children react very differently to whatever form of discipline you use. Mary's had to go back to the drawing board and figure out another way of correcting her baby. Punishment was not going to work, so she tried something different. You have to keep evaluating your form of correction at every stage because what worked when they were toddlers won't work in adolescence. One day instead of being obedient, they will bang the door and roll their eyes. This raises the question, what can you do when correction is no longer received graciously?

1. Evaluate your relationship

How you have been relating to your child will highly dictate how they receive correction. A story comes to mind of an aggressive father who used to beat up his wife when the kids were young. Needless to say that this strained his relationship with his children because they witnessed or heard their mother crying, but they were too young to help.

One day when the son was in high school, his son bullied another child to the point of being suspended from school. His father was furious and tried to slap him when they finally got home. But he did not expect what happened next. His son beat him up, releasing all the years of anger and bitterness he had bottled up over the years. The boy was no longer scared of his father. In fact, he hated him and had no respect for him. What the father thought of as discipline, the son considered it to be a threat, and he defended himself.

It's too late for this father to do anything about his relationship with his kids. However, parents need to first and foremost build a respectful relationship with their children. For a child to receive correction from you, they must respect and hold you in high regard. You must be a father or mother that they admire and love because of what they see in you.

If you come home late from a drunken spree, it is unrealistic to correct your teenage son when they do the same. Monkey see monkey do is the motto of all children. If you don't set an example of a clean house, you don't have the leverage to tell your kids to clean their rooms.

2. Consider their age

How old is your son, and what kind of correction are you using? Are you still hoping that how you disciplined them as toddlers will work when they are 13? Parents need to move with the times and understand that different stages require a different approach.

When a child reaches ten years, you need to start talking to them like an adult while still maintaining your authority. You cannot continue treating them like kids and expect them to respond well. As they grow into teenagers and feel the need to assert themselves, you have to learn negotiating skills. They must clean their rooms and help with the chores if they want to earn an allowance or have their friends over.

3. Put yourself in the child's shoes

Sometimes parents don't stop to consider how a child feels when you are correcting them. A great example is when you correct your child in front of their peers. Just like adults, children have feelings and egos that you should consider. When you correct them publicly, they feel embarrassed and humiliated. They react with anger or what seems to you like aggression, which only gets them into more trouble. You should check where and when you are correcting or disciplining your child so they can receive it.

If a child feels that what they are doing is not wrong in their eyes, you could also face some resistance. For example, small kids learn a lot of things from school and even their friends or the TV. If something they learned from these avenues is considered right, but you say it's wrong, they are likely to disobey you. Parents who have teenagers experience this kind of resistance often when they try to speak against certain hairstyles, tattoos, and piercings. The child will go ahead and do what they want despite your orders, having a firm resolve to deal with the consequences later.

4. Be assertive

Children perform well when there is a clear structure. Give clear guidelines of what is wrong and right. Structure should be established from a very young age and maintained as they grow up. If a parent often says no and then changes their mind, the child will never take them seriously. You must be assertive and let your no be no and your yes be yes.

If you keep giving leeway to the rules you've set, the kids feel unsafe and lose respect for you. It's essential to have clear boundaries and ensure you follow through with what you say.

Children learn to test their parent's limits from a tender age, and it's essential to know when they are doing that. As they come into their teens, they will push these buttons even more just to see what you can allow. It is during these testing periods that you must take authority and be the parent no matter how old the child is.

The Jealousy between siblings and conflicts

Olly had been an only child for five years, she enjoyed her parent's attention and always got anything she wanted. Life was beautiful, except for one thing. When her parents were too tired to play in the evening, she got bored and had nothing to do. She would constantly ask for a sibling but they were not willing to give her one. How fun it would be to have a little sister to play with, or so she thought.

When her parents finally caved in, things took a drastic turn. Her mom no longer had time to play because she was always taking care of her sister who was always crying. She had to wake up at night to keep her little sister calm so everyone else would sleep. Her dad helped occasionally, but sometimes he was too tired to do anything. Besides all the attention her sister took from her, she was also too little to play with.

Olly changed a lot during the first few months. She was withdrawn and cried easily. She started complaining all the time and anger outbursts increased. Her mother, Betty, noticed the change. She was already overwhelmed by the demands of a newborn and could not cope with all the outbursts Olly had lately. What was wrong with her? Why had she changed? She was always so happy before, but now, she was up in arms all the time.

Olly's teacher called Betty one afternoon and asked if they could talk. She would have preferred a meeting but Betty didn't have time. The teacher wanted to talk about the changes that Olly showed for the last few months. She was more withdrawn, cried when she did not know the answer to a question, and she did not want to join the other kids during playtime. According to the teacher, Olly felt neglected now that her little sister was here. She advised that Betty should try and balance the attention.

At first, Betty thought that this was absurd. She gave Olly all the attention she needed, but as time went by, Olly only became worse. Betty called her mother to ask for her opinion. Having raised three kids, she must know what is going on.

"That's easy honey, give her more attention than you do her baby sister. She feels like her sister came to steal you and her father away from her, and if you are not careful, it will develop into a serious rivalry."

Betty decided to try it, after all, scolding Olly had not worked. She started going on icecream dates, movies and spending playtime with Olly. Slowly, she could see her little girl coming back to her. It took some time but reassuring Olly that she was loved and cared for helped get her self-esteem back.

Sibling rivalry can develop from a young age, and while some siblings are lucky to be each other's best friends, some will fight and compete constantly. The cause can be many things, ranging from parental attention, gifts, development stage, and many more. How you handle the conflict determines how soon a lasting solution is found and whether your kids will become friends. How severe the fights get and the factors that mostly lead to the squabbles include the following.

1. **Development stage and evolving needs**

Your kids needs change as they develop and their new anxieties and identities reflect on how they relate with their siblings and others. Toddlers for instance are learning to assert themselves and they become pretty protective of their toys and items. If an older brother or younger sister tries to touch the toys, your toddler is likely to cause a fit. If your child is school going, like Olly, they are very keen on fairness and equality. They will have a hard time understanding all the fuss surrounding their baby sister or brother and might interpret it to mean they are loved less. This

49

becomes a bone of contention and a conflict trigger between siblings.

A teen is learning to be their own person and is developing a sense of independence and individuality. They want to do their own things, at their own pace, without interference from you or anyone else. This will be in direct conflict with house rules, chores, and the help you need from them to care for their younger siblings. How they fight and solve the conflict will highly depend on where your kids are on the development stage.

2. Your kid's temperaments

Every child is unique and their individual personality plays a role in how well they will get along. For instance, one child may be clingy to their parents and need a lot of attention. His or her siblings may, however, resent them because they also want the same amount of attention.

3. How you solve conflicts

Every marriage has problems, and every once in a while you are likely to get into an argument with your partner. How you solve these problems sets an example for your kids on how they should solve their own problems. If you slam doors, shout, call names and break things in the house, your kids are likely to pick up on these bad habits. If you use love, respect, and progressively work towards solving the problems, you are modeling to your kids how they should solve their own conflicts.

4. Lack of structures

Children generally thrive when they have a structure they can follow. Structure refers to having clear rules, expectations, consequences, and routines they need to follow. For instance, when your child comes home from school, what should they do first? What should follow, and how should they proceed after that?

Kids who have no schedule and structure to follow are usually more anxious, and they don't feel safe. They are not grounded by a steady routine which makes it hard for them to know what to expect, fuelling irritability and sibling rivalry. This is done to test the waters so they know what will be acceptable and what won't be tolerated. Once rules and boundaries are set, they settle.

5. No hierarchy among the kids

What time do your kids go to bed? If they are of different ages and go to bed at the same time, sibling rivalry will increase. This is true if the older sibling gets no advantages for being older and more competent. Each child is looking for their own place in the family, so they know where they stand. For instance, an older child wants to know that there are more responsibilities and benefits that come with age so they are inspired to utilize the skills and maturity that come with age.

6. Negative and positive attention

Everyone, even adults want positive attention. If they are denied this attention, the result is to usually shoot for negative, and boy will that get your focus on them. The worst thing is to give them no attention at all. Kids naturally have a high affinity for negative attention, especially when there is little positive attention to go round.

Parents, on the other hand, have a tendency to notice bad behavior more than they do good behavior. These two combined are a ticking time bomb for sibling rivalry, especially where parents constantly compare their kids. The child in question would rather become the 'bad kid' to get the attention they need. One way to pull this off is to have constant squabbles with their siblings.

7. **No problem-solving skills**
Alvin has always complained that his little brother Phil is always messing up his things. He has gone to his parents about it and asked them to keep Phil out of his stuff, but nothing happens. Because he feels like he is not being heard, Alvin has resulted in taking matters into his own hands. This has intensified the rivalry between the two boys.

An easy way to solve this is to settle problems as soon as they arise. Always listen to your kids when they complain and take them seriously. Often, the child who feels ignored ends up feeling like he is not important to you, which leads to depression and low self-esteem.

The connection between sibling rivalry and the lack of confidence in kids

If left unchecked, sibling rivalry can be destructive. Its meant to be a training ground for your kids, a safe environment where they can learn how to cope with disappointment, sharing, taking turns, negotiation, and how to get back up after a defeat. However, it's often the opposite as the kids learn to compete for parental attention.

Each child has different qualities and a unique personality that makes them who they are. As parents, we need to celebrate these qualities and teach the siblings to appreciate each other's strengths. This isn't always the case, and one sibling may get more attention from the outside world than the other. This is despite the parents teaching them how to appreciate each other. If this happens, the balance is often disrupted, resulting in sibling rivalry.

Research has, however, shown that parents are often the cause of this imbalance. Let's take the case of Peter and his little sister Jenny. Although the two are raised by loving and caring parents, Peter suffers from low self-esteem while Jenny is entitled. When they have conflicts, the two kids take the case to their parents, who in all their knowledge, will help them solve the problem.

To be good parents, the kid's mom and dad try to level the field by protecting and supporting Jenny, who is two years younger than Peter. Because of their age difference, Peter is more skilled at playing games, is more mature than his sister, and is also more responsible. However, always taking Jenny's side makes Peter feel like his parents don't love him, don't listen to him, and they definitely only care about Jenny.

The conflicts have escalated, and because he knows his parents will take his sister's side, Peter has stopped trying to get justice. Jenny has noticed the trend. She knows her parents will have her back, and so she picks fights whenever she can. After all, mom and dad will take her side, even when she is wrong. Peter's feelings of inadequacy increase with every battle his sister wins. He often tries to explain the situation to his parents but they always say that Jenny is still a baby. She will outgrow the behavior. He can't wait for her to grow up and stop bothering him.

If left unchecked, this resentment will continue to adulthood and instead of the two being a source of joy and support to each other, they will do whatever it takes to live as far from each other as possible. Sometimes, they will even go to extents not to visit their parents at the same time. If Peter continues with these feelings, he is likely to be a failure in class, relationships, and in his future career and home. He will still feel useless at school, work, and be jealous of his spouse if she gets 'ahead' of him.

The rivalry will be transferred from home to school, career, and into his marriage.

Comparing ourselves to our siblings is normal. We do it all the time, into our adulthood, but when positive feelings are attached to this comparison, we will not be jealous of them, but proud of their achievement. Ok, maybe a little jealous but not to the point of hating them. Which is where the problem comes in. Kids are often threatened when there is a new member of the family. Mom tends to spend more time with the baby, and dad's first stop when he comes home from work is to release mom off her duties so she can rest. Where does that leave them?

A child in this situation, like Olly was, is likely to view their sibling as the cause of all their limitations. If her little sister was not born, her parent's attention would still be hers. It's not surprising that Olly, and others in her situation, will start to compare themselves with their siblings. She is small, that's why she gets all the attention. Subconsciously, Olly will look for ways to make herself small. For instance, she will cry more often, throw tantrums, and in some cases, even pee on herself as her little sister does.

But this behavior won't get her the attention she craves. She will get negative attention, but to her, negative attention is better than no attention at all. You can imagine the disaster this will cause when Olly grows up! She will not only compare her achievements with that of her sister, but she will subconsciously blame her sister for all her misfortunes. No matter how hard she tries, she will feel that she will never measure up, or be as great as her sister, who has already taken that title.

When your child doesn't feel loved

Slam!

That's the last sound Ethan heard before his son screamed he hated him. He was at a loss. He didn't know how this rift had come by, but he was getting desperate to fill it. For the longest time, his son, Aaron, would throw a fit and either say he hated him or accused him of not loving him enough. There is nothing he wants more than for Aaron to believe that he loved him unconditionally, but everything he tried did not work. He was giving up.

We know how much we love our kids, but sometimes, your child will feel unloved. Most of these instances are usually after the child is indisciplined and you try to correct them. They might have broken something or hit their brother with a toy on the head, and when you ask them about it, they accuse you of favoritism, being unfair, or outrightly tell you they hate you and slam the door on your face.

Let's think about Ethan and Aaron for a while. Aaron was busy playing with his toys as his father was busy finishing a project that was needed at work the following morning. As he usually did, he asked Aaron to play somewhere else so he would concentrate on the project. Aaron moved away for a few minutes, but was soon back by his father's side, playing happily and asking his father to see how awesome he was. After absentmindedly telling his 'that's great', he asked Aaron to play somewhere else.

"But you didn't look at my game yet?"
"I will if you let me concentrate on my work. This project is really important." This touches a nerve in Aarons books. He looks at his father, who is still glued to his work, furious.
"More important than me?"
Looking at his son for the first time, Ethan responds. "That's not true. You are the most important person to me. I just need to finish this project and I'm all yours, ok?"
"You'll simply start on another project like you always do!"
By this time, tempers are flying high, and Ethan is not as patient as he would like to be. "If I don't work, what do you think we will eat? Do you want a roof over your head or not?"
"Fine! Finish your important project. I don't care what you do anyway."
"Stop being a brat!"
Aaron storms out and slams the door, shouting how much he hates his father.

Like Aaron, most kids feel unloved because of parental mistakes we make, some unknowingly. Whether it's because our own parents hurt us when we were kids, or it's unintentional oversight, our actions can negatively impact our kids and lowe their self-esteem and confidence. Having kids is more than getting a nursery ready and changing a few diapers. It takes a lot of emotional work for kids to know they are truly loved and safe.

Parental mistakes that make kids feel unloved

1. Unresolved trauma

How our parents treated us will likely be reflected in how we treat our kids. Usually, such cases manifest because parents have no blueprint on how to help their kids when they go through difficult emotional times. You find that the parents were neglected by their own parents and are in turn neglecting their kids. Not because they don't love their kids, but because their emotional blueprint is to push them away. That's what they learned.

These parents also face another roadblock. Because of how their parents treated them, they find it difficult to accept love from children. This directly comes out when they are unable to accept the unconditional love their kids have for them. Because of the emotional pain, it caused them many years ago, they unknowingly inflict the same pain on their kids.

Another parent will, however, overcompensate their lack of experience by over comforting and over-protecting their kids. While this action is done from a place of love, it only reflects as suppressing the child's feelings, which in turn makes the little one feel neglected. The more overprotective and over-comforting the parent is, the more likely they are to be defensive on the child. They will fail to perceive the child correctly and instead of encouraging a healthy relationship and development, they discourage it and instead have kids who lack confidence.

These parents are usually the most confused as to why their kids have low confidence. In their eyes, they are doing the best they can to make their kids feel protected and comforted, but it's not working, which is confusing for them.

2. Allowing your child to cry

There seem to be two contending camps on this issue, but we will clear it out right now. When a child cries or throws a tantrum, they are communicating to you, their primary caregiver, that they are not pleased with something or that they need something. Some parents feel that allowing their kids to cry is teaching them an important life lesson, but we strongly disagree.

When kids are young, the only language they know you can listen to is their crying and fussing. They don't know how to contain their big emotions or how to express them. Because mother nature is all-knowing, she devised crying and tantrums as the best way for babies and toddlers to release this pressure and emotions. Kids have no idea what's happening to them, they're just looking for a way to express themselves.

Imagine the rude shock they get when you, the person who is meant to love them the most in the world, ignore their crying or tantrum! To them, it registers that their needs will not be met, and that you don't care about them. Kids learn not to cry when they need assurance or attention because they know no one is coming to their aid, not because they have learned an 'important' life lesson.

3. Punishment instead of discipline

Kids expect their parents to guide them into being the best they can be. But in the world we grew up in, we became accustomed to punishment and not discipline. Toddlers, for instance, are learning to explore the world around them. They will touch anything and everything as they familiarize themselves with the world and learn about new objects and items.

Punishment does not refer to physically spanking your child only. It refers to time outs and yelling as well. An adult who raised their voice to their little one is traumatizing in the eyes of a child. You usually look like the big bad wolf ready to puff and huff and blow them away. That's not a pretty sight, and any child would do anything to have that smiling, welcoming face back.

When you punish your child, they feel uncared for, and because they don't understand you are trying to teach them a lesson, they think that something is wrong with them. If they were good, you would not punish them. If they did what they were told, they would not get punished. In most cases, this contradicts with the kids development stage. For instance, a toddler who is angry at their friend for not sharing will be tempted to hit the friend. When you punish them, they first feel that emotions are bad because they get them punished, and two, something is wrong with them for feeling angry.

This cycle needs to be stopped and corrected. Our duty as parents is to help our kids understand and manage their emotions, not to punish them for feeling angry, frustrated, and furious. If your child hits a friend for instance, find out why they did it before you take any action. This does not justify hitting others. Far from it. You still need to talk to your child about why hitting is wrong, but once they are calm enough to understand the lesson. In my book on positive parenting, I cover this in detail and explain how kids in each development stage can benefit from positive parenting.

4. You don't talk to your child

Babies are first exposed to language and communication when their parents talk to them. The more parents vocalize to their babies, the more their kids' literacy levels become higher. But talking has another benefit. It makes the child feel connected and loved by their parents. This is so crucial that child development experts say that parents should talk to their infants from day one. It builds a unique and strong relationship between parent and child, and helps develop the child's self-esteem.

Kids who are ignored by their parents feel lonely, detached, and unloved. They are left wondering if something is wrong with them and that's why you are ignoring them. Could it be something they did? The child may even become obsessed with pleasing you, and if you don't notice these efforts, they pull themselves even lower thinking that they will never be good enough.

Kids naturally have lots of questions they want to ask their parents. They will be on your neck every day with questions and stories of how their day was. They rely on you to help them understand concepts they are not sure of and the only way to do that is to ask and talk about it. If you ignore them, they feel lost and their confidence suffers.

5. Present but absent parents

The hustles of life today may be to blame for this, but it should not be an excuse. Sometimes parents come home so tired that they are at home but not available for their kids. Other times, it has nothing to do with being tired. You are just not in the mood to deal with kids. Parents don't get breaks, and your kids will never sit and say "mom is tired, let's keep off until she is in the right mental space to deal with us".

Instead, they will constantly crave your attention and affirmation. They view you as their hero, and when you are there but not available for them, they feel lonely. They have no one to have a heart to heart talk with or share love and affection. This is present but absent parenting, and the result is a child with low self-esteem. If you never tell your children that you love them, if you are always working or using a screen, if you shun physical affection, or if you are depressed and undergo prolonged stress periods, you may be a present but absent parent.

Present but absent parents consistently and persistently communicate to their kids that they are not worth their parent time. This communication is often not done consciously, but kids have a strong intuition and pick up on it immediately. Whether or not you tell them they are a nuisance or simply act like it, the communication your child gets and the effect of this communication is similar.

Chapter Three: Skills

A Child Who Gives Up Too Easily

We live in a harsh world, and with things getting more stringent, kids need to learn all the skills they can get to be successful. Although success has different meanings to different people, the skills required are the same. One of those skills is perseverance and mental strength. Because of their age, kids are naturally impatient, especially when things are not going their way. Because technology has made it possible to get instant gratification, our little one's concentration span and resilience have become even worse.

Why perseverance matters

For a while, Tina watched her daughter struggle with her school project. The little girl was getting so frustrated, and eventually, she abandoned ship and left. In her mind, Tina's daughter was probably wondering why she should continue to struggle with something so frustrating, tedious, or painful.

Studies show that people who persevere in trying circumstances do better in most areas of their lives. Their ability to push through discomfort shows that they have higher IQ, more academic intelligence, and they are better performers at work. Without perseverance, kids like Tina's daughter may grow up to be quitters as adults. They may quit a job because they find it redundant and boring, or because they didn't get the promotion they were eyeing. Their relationships will also suffer because they are likely to end things every time there is a communication breakdown.

Perseverance is a skill like any other. A child who perseveres is confident. They are confident in their ability and know that they can turn things around, even when they don't work out at first. Teaching them these skills is helping them improve their concept of self and become comfortable in their ability. Like confidence, perseverance is an abstract concept that kids may not understand, but it's possible to help kids develop this skill. But first, let us examine why kids give up easily.

1. They are embarrassed

Kids are growing, and during this time, they will encounter a lot of situations that leave them feeling dumb. For instance, Tina's daughter might have thought she knew exactly how to go about her school project, but once she encountered a challenge, she realized that maybe she does not know as much as she thought she does. If she takes this too seriously, she will condemn herself for being dumb and feel embarrassed that she does not know what to do.

This happens mostly when kids try to bite more than they can chew. If the school project involves a lot of things, Tina's daughter would have had a better chance if she did not look at the project as a whole, but divided it into different actionable sections. But kids don't do this. In their minds, they have a project that needs to be completed. Sometimes, looking at the project from this perspective can be so overwhelming for them that they don't start. That is, giving up even before they start.

2. Your expectations are high

At every stage of development, kids have tasks they can handle and those they can't no matter how much they try. Always check if the job you are giving your child is age-appropriate. Toddlers may help clear the table, but setting it might be complicated for them. You should shift your expectations to fit what your child can and cannot do. This will help build their confidence.

The opposite is also true. Sometimes, parents shield their kids so much that they fail to give them age-appropriate tasks. For example, pre-teens can help with a lot of chores in the house. They can arrange their closets, cook an egg, and even help with cleaning the house. Kids who are willing to help often suffer when their parents refuse to give them responsibilities. Using a knife may be dangerous, but a pre-teen can handle themselves with care and help you chop some tomatoes.

3. Putting too much emphasis on winning

Winning is good, and there is nothing wrong with it, but, when we emphasize winning too much, it takes away the fun from the activity. Also, our kids feel like losers unless they are undefeated. This also happens in class and while doing homework. There is nothing wrong with being competitive, but when game night turns into a teary affair because your child didn't win, then you need to help them check their expectations. The process should be as enjoyable as the game. Teach your kids to appreciate the process as much as they appreciate winning. If they didn't win, they will have had fun.

4. Generic praise

When kids do something great, we naturally want to praise them and show them we appreciate their effort. However, simply saying "good girl" and "good boy" or "excellent" is traditionally what parents say to their kids. What we don't realize is that "good boy" can easily be undermined by "bad boy," which confuses the child. Is he a good boy or a bad boy? If he hears you tell him that he's a bad boy more than he hears good boy, it registers in his mind that he is a bad boy. On special occasions, he is a good boy. This lowers his confidence.

5. You don't help with emotions

Big emotions are overwhelming for kids, and when they don't understand them, they become frustrated and confused. Emotions such as anger and frustration are often the ones that make us tick. An angry child will yell, hit others, throw a fit, and do whatever it takes to feel better. This behavior does not sit well with parents, and the likelihood of losing our cool is high. And when we do, we become the big bad wolf.

Another challenge that this causes is that when we lose control, we are unable to help our kids with their emotions. Like Aaron and his father, emotions fly high, and the results are a slammed door, and two angry people. Although we should not encourage kids to hit, yell, and shout, we must understand that this is their way of expressing their emotions. However, we must always talk to them about what is appropriate behavior and what is unacceptable.

One of the best ways to deal with this is to help kids name the emotions they are feeling. This shows them that feelings are part of life, but it also communicates that these feelings have a name and a proper way to express them. We must help them name the emotion so that they learn what it is they are feeling. Next time your child cries, ask them if they are sad or feeling frustrated.

How to build resilience in kids

Stacy has been picking Tom from school for a while. Things have improved, and he seemed to be doing a lot better. Today, however, she notices that something is off from the moment Tom walks out of the school. He must be upset about something.

"What's wrong, buddy? Are you ok?"

"I got a role in the school play."

"That's wonderful! Congratulations!"

"No! No! No! It's not wonderful!"

"Why not?"

"The drama teacher is making me play a girl!" and he bursts into tears.

At this point, Stacy is tempted to laugh, but she understands that her son's emotions are real. He is disappointed, and she acknowledges that. But she keeps quiet.

1. Go against your natural instincts

Any parent's first instinct would be to talk to Tom about why the situation is not so bad. You would be tempted to come up with three to four reasons why he should not be disappointed, why this is a great opportunity, and even add how much fun it would be. That's our natural instinct. When we chill with our friends, that's what we do. But the truth is, we talk too much! We tend to explain, analyze, and rationalize everything. Which is the exact opposite of what our kids need.

Children can't hear or process information, tactics, and processes when they are upset. And to be honest, neither can you. Think of a time you were upset about something, and all you wanted to do was vent. If someone told you you shouldn't be upset because of 1, 2, and 3, or what a wonderful learning experience it was, it might upset you further rather than make you feel better. So, why do we do this to our kids?

Sitting with your child when they are upset shows that you love them, you respect what they are feeling, and you are ready to offer them a shoulder to cry on. It's incredibly hard for parents to do because our natural instinct is to protect our little ones. But if we want the best results, we must learn to swim against the current.

2. Stop saving the day

How many times have you wanted to save the day when your child came home upset? Stacy, for instance, could have decided to talk to the drama teacher and ask him to change Tom's role. Would it have made Tom happy? Absolutely! But it would have taught him that his mother will always be there to save him when unpleasant things happen to him.

Instead of being a super mom, Stacy can use this opportunity to help Tom develop some internal grit. Resilience is developed when we don't quit at first sight of a challenge. To encourage him, she can tell Tom that directors start by awarding smaller roles, but when they see how good an actor is, they can easily swap the role with something more meaningful. If the actor's attitude is positive, it makes the process even easier. Also, the opportunity to make new friends has just been presented. It would be fun to get to know some of the other boys and girls in the play and have fun while at it.

Challenges are a test to your child's emotional immune system. When a healthy body catches a virus, tons of antibodies are produced to help fight the 'enemy' and the body becomes stronger. The same happens with resilience. The more your child overcomes challenges, the tougher they grow, and the more confident they are that they can solve whatever difficulty they face.

3. Breakdown the goals

When kids start a project, it's usually all fun until they encounter a roadblock. Let's assume you brought a new puzzle home, and although your little one is excited to give it a go, they are not sure where to start. It's a new challenge for them, and the pieces are much smaller than the ones he is accustomed to. If you notice they are tempted to give up, you could help them breakdown the task by asking them if they prefer to look for the corners first. Once that's done, you can move to the edges.

4. Give failure a new meaning

Everyone, including adults, fears falling short. That's completely understandable, but the way life is designed, we are bound to fail every so often. You must talk to your child about failure, and give it a new meaning. If they are learning how to spell, tell them it's natural to get it wrong the first few times, but the more they practice, the better they become. This helps them appreciate the process and enjoy the sweet victory that comes with persistence. Your child will also get a lot of experience with win/lose situations, which will give them the confidence they need to keep trying even when they know they might fail.

5. Use the batman effect

A study conducted on child development shows that asking kids to pretend to be Batman, Dora the Explorer, or other hard-working characters they admire can significantly help them increase their confidence and resilience. The research found that asking kids to embody the characteristics of a hard-working, confident, resilient character helped them get through the task. These kids were less stressed and managed to perform the task better than kids who referred to themselves. Next time your child is about to give up, remind him how batman was in the same situation, and help him remember how batman made it through. Then ask him to be batman and to use batman powers to do the task.

6. Model the character

Kids naturally do what they see us do, not what we tell them to do. Allowing your kids to see you struggle with tasks and not give up shows them that they too can handle the challenges they face. Openly tell them when something seems difficult for you, but assure them you will not give up. Once you manage, celebrate with them. This could be anything from learning to cook using a new recipe, learning how to play a musical instrument or a project at work.

Your child is a perfectionist and too self-critical

One night while John's seven-year-old son Ethan was doing his homework, he pointed out that Ethan had written the number five backward. What happened next was entirely unexpected. Ethan threw himself on the floor, banging his fists as he whined, saying how he couldn't do it right. John got him to calm down and try again, but when he still couldn't do it, Ethan gave up in a huff and went to his bedroom.

Does this sound familiar? If so, chances are your child is a perfectionist. You have heard parents bragging how their little ones stayed up all night to complete one task. You can even hear some refer to their kids as perfectionists. However, any parent who thinks perfectionism is a status symbol does not understand how this trait could be a serious problem.

If you have or are raising a perfectionist, you have probably seen firsthand how difficult it can be. Torn up papers, late nights, and tantrum episodes are just some of the behaviors you may have witnessed in the budding perfectionist.

Perfectionism is an attempt to control circumstances that make the child uncomfortable. Perfectionists get some short-term relief from this control. Top achievers are motivated by doing their best, and while setbacks can be painful, they are not too bothered by them. Perfectionists, on the other hand, are driven by the fear of failure and a desire to be accepted. They view mistakes as proof that they are not good enough. Recent studies have shown that anxiety is the root cause, and genetics play some part in it. Some kids, however, are pressured to be perfect by their parents and society.

Whether your kid melts down whenever she makes a mistake during basketball practice, or she spends hours every day trying to find the perfect outfit, perfectionism takes a toll on children's lives. It can affect their well being and also put a strain on their relationships. This self-criticism can lead to low self-esteem, and frequent frustrations can result in tantrums and power struggles. And this can stress out everyone involved. If left unchecked, it can have lifelong consequences.

What behavior can be considered as perfectionism?

It is good for kids to have high expectations of themselves, but if they expect to be perfect, they will never be satisfied with their performance. Perfectionists set unrealistic goals for themselves and place a lot of pressure on themselves to try and achieve their goals. For them, it is all-or-nothing. Most kids would be proud of scoring a 99 on a test or scoring 7 out of 10, but to a perfectionist, this is a foul shot. Perfectionists view their performance as a dismal failure when they fall short of their goals even by just 1.

You would think that when they achieved their goals, it would be okay, but they often struggle to enjoy their accomplishments. They choke it up to good luck and worry they won't be able to replicate the results or maintain their level of success. This fear thing can lead them to give up on tasks or avoid doing them altogether. This keeps them from reaching their full potential.

Ethan's younger brother can easily start breakdancing in front of everyone, but Ethan would never do that. He is too worried about being laughed at. He wants to do things right or not do them at all.

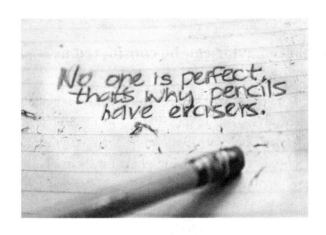

Types of Perfectionism

Some researchers believe someone can be an adaptive perfectionist. This means that a child's unrealistically high expectations could actually serve him well in life. But others argue that true perfectionism is always dangerous. Three distinct types of perfectionism have been identified:

1. Self-Oriented Perfectionists – they hold unrealistic expectations for themselves
2. Other-Oriented Perfectionists – they set unrealistic standards for other people
3. Socially-Prescribed Perfectionists – they believe that other people, such as their parents or coaches, have set unrealistic expectations of them.

All three kinds of perfectionism can be harmful to a child's well-being. Before you help your child overcome perfectionism, you must first know if they are perfectionists.

Signs that your child might be a perfectionist

The warning signs of perfectionism will vary depending on your kid's age and the kind of perfectionism he experiences. But, generally, symptoms may include high sensitivity to criticism and difficulty finishing assignments because it is never 'good enough.' Procrastinating to avoid doing difficult tasks and being too self-critical, self-conscious, and easily embarrassed. Perfectionists are very critical of other people and have trouble making decisions or prioritizing tasks. They also exhibit a low frustration tolerance for mistakes and high anxiety when failure happens. Scientists think these factors may contribute to perfectionism in children

1. Biological factors

Studies conducted in 2015 show that perfectionism is closely linked to certain mental illnesses, such as OCD (obsessive-compulsive disorder) and some eating disorders. This leads the scientists to conclude that there may be a biological component to perfectionism.

2. Parental influences

Most parents praise their children when they achieve something. Honoring your child's achievements too much can lead them to believe that mistakes are bad and that she should succeed at all costs.

3. Perfectionist parents

Perfectionist parents are more likely to raise perfectionist children. The perfectionism can stem from learned behavior if the child sees a parent's quest for perfection or may also reflect a genetic disposition.

4. Academic pressures

Children may fear to get less than perfect test scores because they can sabotage their efforts of getting into a good college. Those academic pressures can cause them to feel like they need to be perfect all the time to get anywhere in life.

5. The sensationalism of success and failure

The media often portrays successful people as perfect. At the same time, they also show how one mistake can cause someone to become a complete failure. These stories can influence young people to think that they need to be perfect at everything they do if they want to succeed.

6. Desire to please

Kids often attempt to gain admiration and affection by showing they can be perfect in every way. This can stem from a need to reduce a parent's stress, or it may be the only way they know how to get attention.

7. Low self-worth

A kid who feels terrible about himself may think he's only as good as his achievements. Perfectionists tend to focus on their mistakes and minimize their accomplishments, which prevents them from ever feeling good enough.

8. Trauma

Traumatic experiences may cause children to feel like they are unloved or that they won't be accepted unless they are perfect.

Potential dangers of Perfectionism

Being a perfectionist will not help your child rise to the top. In fact, it may have the opposite effect. The anxiety they get over making mistakes can prevent them from succeeding. Their fear of failure keeps them from trying new things if there is a possibility of failure. Perfectionist children often mask their pain and turmoil. They feel compelled to appear perfect on the outside, and consequently, many suffer silently when problems arise because they don't want to be seen as weak. Perfectionism can lead to mental health problems as they are at a higher risk for depression, anxiety, and other mental health issues.

They also experience higher levels of stress than other kids their age. Since perfectionists feel compelled to avoid mistakes, they're under more pressure all the time. And too much stress can be bad for a person's physical, mental, and emotional health.

How to address perfectionism in children

If you notice any of the warning signs that your child may be a budding perfectionist, there are several things you can do to help. Here are some strategies for addressing perfectionism.

1. Commend your child's efforts rather than the outcome

    Instead of praising your child for scoring a 100 on her spelling test, praise her for studying hard. You can also applaud her for being kind to others or for being a good friend. Make it clear that achievement isn't the only important thing in life.

2. Share your own failures

    Make it clear to your child that you aren't perfect, and they shouldn't try to be. Tell him about the time you didn't get a job or a time when you failed a test and explain how you coped with your failure.

3. Teach healthy coping skills

    Although failure is uncomfortable, it's not intolerable. Teaching your child how to deal with disappointment, rejection, and mistakes in a healthy way can go a long way in improving their quality of life. Suggest different coping methods such as talking to a friend, or writing in a journal to help deal with their feelings.

4. Encourage and teach them healthy self-talk

Teach your child to use self-compassion as opposed to self-criticism. Talk to yourself out loud to show your child that you can treat yourself with kindness even when you make mistakes. Don't say negative things about yourself or fixate on your mistakes; instead, model positive self-esteem for your child. By telling them factual or fictional stories about how you got over your mistakes, you are showing them non-anxious ways of coping and giving them an example of more realistic self-talk.

5. Make things clear

Catching yourself while making a negative statement can create a valuable teaching moment. Say you burn the cookies you were making and yell in frustration that you are a lousy cook. If your child is around don't stop the conversation there, continue with something like, "well am not a bad cook, I'm pretty good one most of the time, I just messed up this time, and I'm not going to let that stop me from making cookies in the future."

6. Monitor your expectations

Ensure that you are not putting too much pressure on your child to be perfect. Instead, set high but reasonable expectations for them. Also, monitor your expectations overtime to ensure that you aren't expecting too much from your child. If he fails to meet your goals or your child wants to quit trying to reach your goals, you may be expecting too much from him. Help your child identify what he can and what he can't control.

Whether it is being the best player on the basketball team or acing every test, it is important to let your child know that she cannot control many of the circumstances that influence his success. He can't control how hard the teacher makes his tests, and he can't control how well his peers perform, but he can control his effort.

7. Set realistic goals with your child.

Talk to your child about the goals he wants to achieve. If his goals require perfection, talk to him about the dangers of setting unrealistically high goals for herself, and help him find more realistic ones.

8. Help your child acquire healthy self-esteem

Engage in activities that help your child feel good about who he is, not just what he accomplishes. Volunteering, learning new things, and engaging in artistic endeavors are just a few ways to help your child develop a healthier view of himself.

9. When to get professional help

When your child's perfectionism is causing them social problems, it might be time to seek professional advice. For example, if your child refuses to socialize because he's on a quest to get a perfect grade. He may put off making friends to focus on his academic goal. In the long run, he will need professional help to reassimilate into society.

Learning problems can be another warning sign that your child may benefit from speaking to a mental health professional. For example, if your child can't finish projects because he thinks his work isn't good enough or he rips up his papers whenever he makes a mistake. Talking to a professional may help figure out how to deal with this situation.

If you are worried that your child is a perfectionist, talk to your child's primary care physician. Discuss the signs that you are seeing and share how those issues impact your child's life. A physician can refer your child to a mental health professional for an assessment. If treatment is needed, your child may benefit from therapy to reduce her perfectionism and feelings of self-criticism.

Chapter Four: Choice

What to do if he can never decide

A couple of months ago, as I was pushing my trolley in the grocery store, I saw a kid screaming and kicking while the mother just stood and watched him. It turns out the mom tried to buy ice-cream for this little boy. Unfortunately, there were six flavors, and he couldn't decide which one he wanted. What followed was a huge fight between the mom and the frustrated boy who ended up with no ice-cream.

The inability to make simple decisions is very common with young kids. The choice between eggs and cereal for breakfast, basketball or football at school and even what toy to pick in the store can become a one hour struggle. At a young age, when you can decide for him these things, it may not seem like a big deal. But soon, he will have to decide on a course, a college, a spouse, and even a house or a car. Life presents us with choices every day, and only fast decision-makers thrive.

The author of The Paradox of Choice, Barry Schwartz, categorizes people into two groups; maximizers and satisficers. Maximizers are people who always analyze and scrutinize to make the best decision while satisficers quickly pick what seems good enough. While the maximizer spends hours and even days trying to make a decision, the satisficer has already dealt with the consequences of whatever decision they made and moved on to the next thing.

Importance of Learning to Make Decisions as a Young Child

Have you ever met a lady who takes all their clothes from the closet to the bed every morning in order to decide what they are going to wear on that day? It's not a surprise that this lady is always late, and when she arrives, she is flustered.

Another example is a guy who strings along with several girls because he can't pick one. It's easy to blame these two people and even call them names. However, this indecisiveness often stems from their childhood. Their parents did not take the time to train them on the importance of choice. The parent either decided for them or just left them alone to deal with their demons.

The ability to make a choice quickly has everything to do with confidence. It's your job as a parent to build that confidence in your child so that they can grow up with it. In the examples above, these two people face real struggles every day when faced with choices. As a result, they are hurting themselves and others because they can't decide.

Fortunately, the decisions kids have to make don't have serious consequences. This is the most appropriate time to train a child to be a quick but smart decision-maker. Before looking at what you can do to help your child makes decisions, let's see what are some of the things that contribute to this inability of making decisions;

1. Fear of failure

Fear of failure is the most plausible reason why a child spends a significant amount of time going back and forth. They don't want to make the wrong decision. From birth, human beings know that every choice comes with a consequence, and nobody wants to deal with bad consequences. 'What if I pick basketball and I'm not good at it?' 'If I take my time to decide, I won't make a wrong decision.'

As a parent, let your child know that it's okay to make mistakes because that's how you learn. If they are big enough to understand, tell them that you also make mistakes and then correct them later. So what if they are not good at basketball? They can always change to something else in the future. Try to discourage perfectionism because it can be very paralyzing for a child and even as an adult.

Failure to make a decision is a choice in itself that always leads to failure. They cannot passively go through life without deciding where their life is headed. You have to train your child to make a choice whichever way it goes. Maybe you can teach them to look at the pros and cons if something is important, but at the end of the day, making a choice is what really matters.

2. Too many choices

A child cannot process many things at the same time. When you are at the store, and you ask them to choose between an entire aisle of toys or snacks, it's normal for them to get overwhelmed. They will go from one end to the other, looking at all the possibilities in front of them and imagining what their lives would be like if they have all those things. Your child knows that they can't have all of it, and that brings an emotional aspect to decision making.

You should also not ask kids open-ended questions like "what would you like to have for dinner?" A child's mind doesn't have the capacity to think about such complicated things.

What you can do to make a choice more manageable is to narrow down the options. For example, choose between yogurt and milkshake or Legos and a toy car and let them decide between the two. Present your child with less overwhelming choices so their little brains won't crash and burn.

3. Fear of parents reaction

Kids are terrified of bad reactions from their parents. When you burst out in rage, your child curls up in fear, and they never want to deal with that again. Due to time constraints, most parents look at their child right in the face and tell them to choose between orange juice and mango juice. When they pause a little, the parent screams at them to just pick. While this may look like it's helping, it actually does the opposite. Your child will choose anything just to avoid your angry fit. Most of the time, however, the child will start crying instead of choosing.

Your job as a parent is to always stay calm in a storm however hard this is. Instead of shouting at them, give them a few seconds to decide. You can then follow up with some reassurance that whatever decision they make will be fine because they are both good. For example, you can say, 'just choose one, and then tomorrow you can try this other one.' That will help them know that what is essential at that point is to make a choice, and then you can correct it later if you don't like it.

4. Poor self-image

Inability to make a decision is one of the signs of low self-esteem. This child thinks that they are stupid, so they don't feel confident enough to make a decision. They second guess everything they do, even simple things like choosing between one and two in an exam. When this child looks at other people, they think that making decisions for them is easy, so they feel even more stupid and inadequate.

As a parent or a teacher dealing with such a child, it's good to be open with them. Let the child know that decision making doesn't come easy to you too. Give them examples of how you couldn't decide where to go to school or what course to take in college.

Assure them that they are brilliant, and what they are going through is not unique to them. Then help them to decide on something and then another and then another until they start to gain confidence.

5. Fear of loss

When you pick one over the others, it means you have to let go of all the other options. This is a concept many kids have trouble dealing with. They do realize that they can't have everything, so it's hard to let go of the others.

This feeling is completely understandable, even in adults. What you can do to help them is to assure them that they can pick something else next time. If today you can only get strawberry ice-cream, next time you can choose vanilla and then the other time blueberry. The anticipation of 'til next time' will make the loss more bearable so they can pick an item.

Other Methods to help your child make decisions

1. Flip a coin

When dealing with autistic children, teachers tell them to flip a coin when making decisions. This takes the pressure of the child to choose between this and that. At this young age, decisions are not life and death, and all they have to do is just pick one over the other. Say cereal is heads and eggs are tails and then throw the coin in the air. Alternatively, play 'inky, pinky ponky' and choose one. It's an enjoyable and easy way to make decisions, but with time you have to train them critical thinking because it won't always be that easy.

2. Take the choice away from them

'I will count to 20 and then choose for you if you will not decide'. This is one of the most effective methods to help a child make a choice. They want to feel that what they are eating or playing with was their choice and not yours, so they won't let you get to 20. However, you have to be very casual and playful about this because if you intimidate them, they will curl up in fear in fear and let you decide instead.

3. Evaluate your verbal and physical demeanor

Most of the time, parents stand over their kids and ask them to make a choice. Have you ever thought how intimidating this can be for that child looking up at your giant body?

Children cannot process many things at the same time. At this point, their little minds are dealing with how big and scary you are instead of what you are saying.

Try to squat and come down to their level with a smile on your face. Then you can ask them to choose one in a relaxed way. They will quickly read your facial cues and see that it's not threatening and then focus one the decision at hand.

4. Be an example

Children learn from what they see from other people, but mostly their parents. One of the ways you can help a child is to take them along in your decision making train. For example, when you are grocery shopping, take them with you. Stand in the fruit aisle and model verbally how to choose between this fruit and that one. If you are shopping for clothes, let them watch the process you go through to make a choice.

When you and your spouse are deciding on which school he should go to, let him sit in on that conversation and listen to the pros and cons of those choices. You can even let him give his two cents and be sure to take them seriously. As a model, you have to be a good decision-maker to avoid confusing the kid even more. Don't make it look too easy that they are intimidated but also don't take too long to decide.

5. Resist the hero mentality

If your child is really struggling to make decisions, you may get irritated and make the choice for them. For some, their kids make really terrible choices, so they step in with their hero cape on and save the day. What this hero mentality will do is make your child weak and lower their self-confidence.

If you have ever landed in a new city for college or work, you know it can feel overwhelming because you don't know the place. When you get lost, you stand and choose between going left or right because there is no one to hold your hand. Eventually, as a result of getting lost, you figure out the entire city.

The same applies to kids. You have to allow them to figure things out and face the consequences of their choices. Next time they will make a better choice because they have learned the hard way. This is how your child gets the confidence they need to navigate this world because you worked out their decision-making muscles.

The art of making decisions is not something that comes naturally to most children. You have to train them slowly and patiently. Practice makes perfect, and with each choice, they make their confidence goes up. Resist the urge to be critical or save them unless it's a matter of life and death.

What to do when your child feels different from other

A few years ago, we had our ten-year high school reunion. As we stood with my high school friends scanning the room to check out some of the guys, we noticed a strange lady.

"who is that?" Maggie asked.

"I don't know," Jane replied as the rest of us concurred.

It turns out, this lady, whose name was Naomi, was actually in our class for the entire four years, but none of us ever noticed her. Even on the night of the reunion, she stood out because she was sitting alone in a corner, sipping her drink.

This is the story of many kids who feel different and isolated as they go through life. While some cases are not as extreme as Naomi's, kids who are shy, artistic, or have developmental challenges tend to get isolated by their peers unintentionally.

Humans are social beings, so they desire to be part of a social circle. Unfortunately, the world does not take uniqueness very kindly. For you to fit in at school or work, you have to be a regular person with what people consider to be typical personalities. Woe unto you if you are unique in behavior, thoughts, dressing, and even talent-wise.

Reasons Why Kids Feel Different

1.   Low self-esteem

When a child has a poor self-image, it manifests in the way they carry themselves, socialize with others and the things they do. Sometimes low self-esteem can manifest itself as shyness where a child chooses to look down and never face people. Other times, the child will isolate themselves from others for fear of rejection. When a child feels that other people are better, smarter, more beautiful than them, they think they have nothing to offer the world, so they hold back. Low self-esteem stems from a young age, and it can be contributed by parents, siblings, and even teachers.

2.   Artistic mind

People with creative minds like musicians, comedians, and writers tend to struggle to fit in when they are young. Their brains don't work the way other people's minds do. When a comedian sees something mundane, immediately, their mind makes up a joke. Before a child grows up to know that this is a unique talent that will make you a gift to the world, they feel different and weird. When Madonna was a child, she used to stand on tables and sing at the top of her lungs.

This didn't go so well with the teachers at the time because they thought she was impulsive.

3. Autism

Autism spectrum disorder is a condition that is characterized by poor social skills, repetitive behavior, and speech problems. As a result, these kids do feel very different from others and they tend to isolate themselves. Unfortunately, their peers may make fun of them and even harass them because of their challenges.

4. Developmental problems

Unlike autism, which is easier to diagnose at a young age, some kids go through some developmental challenges that no one notices until it's too late. For example, a child who continually performs poorly in class and never seems to get anything can be called stupid. However, they may have learning problems such as Dyslexia. While other kids laugh at them, the parent and the teachers reprimand him for failing, adding more salt to the wound.

5. Sexual confusion

It is easier to assume that kids are born as girls or boys. Unfortunately, it's not that simple for some children. Today, there are many stories of kids who committed suicide because of sexual confusion.

They feet like girls in a boy's body and didn't know what to do with that, or they are attracted to the same sex.

A few years ago, an 11-year-old tried to harm themselves because all the kids in their school thought he was peculiar. This boy's behavior and the way he carried himself were very girlish, which caused the taunting even from his father, who kept telling him to man up.

Religious groups are often quick to reprimand these types of kids and ignore their concerns, but that only makes the problem worse. What that child is feeling is legitimate and challenging to deal with, so they should be handled with care.

6. Physical looks

Unfortunately, kids have learned to judge one another based on looks. For example, kids make fun of those who have crooked teeth and lazy eyes. Pop culture has not helped either because it portrays perfection in the form of thin girls with long legs. If your child is a bit on the thick side or they wear spectacles or braces on their teeth, they will likely feel different and shunned by others. If their taste in clothes is not what is considered fashionable at the time, you can expect that they will be made fun of.

Understanding why your child feels different is crucial to finding a solution to their problem. If a child is being taunted for being stupid, finding out they have dyslexia will help you to find a solution to that issue. If they are attracted to same-sex or feel like they don't belong in their bodies, counseling and other hormonal treatments can help them to feel normal again.

However, the only way to know your child is to spend a lot of quality time with them. Just hang out and talk, foster a very close friendship so they can feel free to talk to you. Always try to hold your judgment or criticism and instead take a sympathetic approach first.

How to Help a Child Who Feels Different

1.   Listen to them

When a child comes to their parents to say that they don't fit in, usually, the first response is to minimize the issue or blame someone. Sometimes, a child needs to be heard by the person who matters most to them. Try to control your facial cues and even your mouth from speaking and judging. Let them talk, and you can occasionally affirm what you are hearing them say. The first step to understanding what this child is going through is to listen to their side of the story.

After you listen keenly, you can then reassure your child and offer some help. For example, you can say, 'I am so sorry you are going through this, and it sometimes happens to a lot of kids, but we will find a solution together.'

2.   Don't overreact

When the child tells you that the other kids in school don't want to play or talk to them, what do you do? Do you roll out in tears and breakdown, or do you get up in rage and rush to the school to fix the issue?

None of these reactions is okay or helpful. You have to stay calm and deal with your child, first in a loving and non-reactive way. Try to find out why they feel the other kids are doing that, what your child feels and how they think you can help. You can then start a journey of finding a solution to that problem together through counseling, coaching, and social skills.

3.   Start with just one friend

Researchers show that people need one good friend to survive this world. Instead of trying to get your child to fit in with the crowd, start with helping them to foster just one quality friendship. It could be with their desk mate, another child who is facing the same problem in school or a neighbor outside school. You have to show them how to make friends and take the leap instead of retreating to their secluded corner.

4. Celebrate their uniqueness

For some weird reason, being unique and different is considered to be a drawback in this world. However, you need to let your child know that being different is a good thing. You can do this at home by celebrating their uniqueness. Let them showcase what they have to offer and then have fun as a family.

You can also go a step further and research famous people who have the same uniqueness as your child and show them that. For example, some of the most prominent billionaires in the world, like Bill Gates and Henry Ford, had Dyslexia, and kids made fun of them. Bill Gates's case was so bad that he dropped out of school.

Help them to know that what makes them different is what will make them successful in life. However, be sure to manage their egos, so they don't go around telling people that they will be billionaires like Bill Gates and get a beating.

5. Bring out their inner joy and talents

All children have something unique and interesting they can offer the world. Mother Nature put a genius in every child that should be the basis of finding fulfillment and purpose in your life. Artistic, autistic, and those children who are considered queer have especially great talents they are hiding.

As a parent, it's your job to bring out those talents and gifts from within them. A child who is considered a geek can be a world chess champion. A child whose mind is creative can be the next Madonna or Trevor Noah. When the child is doing that which brings them fulfillment, they will not feel different anymore, and crowds of people will be camping around them to see the talent.

6.   Match them to a role model

A few years ago, a kid who was born with no limbs had the privilege of meeting the famous Nick Vujicic. The world-renowned motivational speaker and preacher challenged this boy to a football match. Needless to say that this child's life took a turn for the better because Nick showed him that being born without limbs is not a limitation. Similarly, matching your child with a role model who has faced a similar issue can help to motivate them to break the barrier and rise above it.

7.   Build their self-esteem

All the problems of life stem from how you feel on the inside. If you feel good about yourself and your approach to life is positive, nothing and no one will ever bring you down. However, when you feel worthless, less than, stupid, short, you will always think that's how other people see you. The first thing a parent needs to do is to repair their child's self-esteem so they can have the tenacity to deal with the world.

Spend a lot of time with that child reassuring them of their worth. Use resources that can help you build their self-worth and become confident people. The reality is, confident people, attract others while timid people repel others. Your child needs to recognize that their uniqueness is a strength, not a weakness, and use it for good. If a child has dyslexia, they are probably outstanding in football, so harness that to the fullest. If they have autism, they are probably excellent artists. Teach your child to focus on what they can do instead of what they cannot.

If physical looks are the reason why your child feels different, there is not much you can do except teaching them to accept who they are. Let them know that those people are the problem, not them. When a classmate kept pulling and making fun of my long brown hair, the teacher told me that they do that because they are jealous. All the while, I thought there was something wrong with having brown hair instead of black. That comment from the teacher made the teasing all more bearable, and when she made fun of it, I just smiled inside.

Bullying

Children who are different and unique may face isolation for most of their childhood, and that is okay. However, if the other kids are bullying them in any way, it's time to step up as a parent and intervene. Bullying could be in the form of being beaten up, taking their stuff, being harassed and mistreated, and even online bullying. If you get wind of such instances, you should head to the school and have the parents of the other kids called and even the police. Bullying must be stopped from the onset and serious consequences handed out to the bullies so they can learn.

Chapter Five: How to Help Your Child Build Their Confidence

Living with bullying and other problems

Most kids have gone through teasing and it's usually harmless if done in with a light touch. But at times lines are crossed, and the things being done or said become hurtful. If bullying was a way of life, then it would not be a concern, but sadly the victims carry the consequences into adulthood.

Bullying is a form of aggression that can take many faces. It could be physical abuse such as hitting or shoving. It can also be verbal, where the bully calls the victim embarrassing names, mocks, or threatens them. Psychological torture is also another form of bullying which can be done by spreading rumors aimed at hurting the victim. Bullies also take advantage of technology and attach other kids through text messages and social media. This is called cyber-bullying.

Parent's often find it difficult to tell when their kids are victims of bullying. Mostly, it's the child who tells the parent that someone is picking on them.

If things are really bad, the parent will notice physical marks on their child. That is why, as a parent, it is necessary to pay attention to your kid's behavioral patterns and any concerns they have. Due to the adverse effects of bullying, such as suicides or school shootouts, it ought to be recognized and dealt with early.

Luckily, there are warning signs you can look out for to tell if your kid is a victim of bullying. If your child seems withdrawn, moody, or anxious take time to ask them if they are ok. If they are no longer interested in activities they considered fun, such as computer games or taking the bus to school, something could be up. Sometimes, kids come back with damaged items and a child who was not a bedwetter starts wetting their bed or having restless nights.

Kids don't talk about bullying immediately. To them, being a victim of bullying is embarrassing and sometimes they are afraid of what might happen if you find out. For instance, parents often talk to the school about such cases, which often makes the situation worse for their child. Although they know you mean, they are afraid things will only get worse if they speak up. Opening the communication lines is the best way to get your child talking. Find a subtle way to bring up the topic. You can ask indirect questions such as:

- Tell me one thing you enjoyed doing today and one thing that made you feel bad?
- Have you ever witnessed bullying?
- What do you think bullying is?
- What should you do if someone bullies you or a friend?

You should be ready to address their concerns or questions with answers that are befitting. Give them strategies on how they can deal with bullying. Some actions they can take may include:

- Calmly telling the bully to stop
- Walking away from the situation
- Avoiding areas where they feel unsafe
- Talking to a trusted grown-up about what happened
- They should not fight back or resort to bullying because it can quickly turn violent

In addition to helping them deal with the situation, it is critical that the child feels safe. Bullying can affect the child negatively; the child needs to know that he is loved and heard so that he grows into a confident being.

What if your child is the bully? It may come as a shock to discover that your child is the one responsible for the pain of another kid. It's difficult to process that you have a bully for a child, but this is often a cry for help for most kids. You must take action to stop the behavior immediately before it escalates to an ingrained habit and grows with your child to adulthood. In most cases, a bully is unable to form sustainable relationships or is trying different personalities before they settle on who they want to be. Their schoolwork is often affected by this behavior, which only makes it worse..

There are many reasons why kids bully others. For instance, they feel insecure, or they are unable to deal with their own emotions. Some kids don't know that it is wrong to pick on others simply because their race, body shape, or accent is different. For some children, it's a result of the behaviors they pick from home. Regular exposure to aggression and cruel acts is more likely to produce a child that does the same to other kids because that is what they deem usual behavior.

How to help your child overcome bullying

1. Listen to your child

Most kids are not afraid of talking about bullying. They will openly tell you what is happening and the form of bullying they are facing. Before you react and jump into action, first offer a listening ear to your child and understand what they are going through. Reacting too strongly may hinder your child from sharing what they are going through. Also, don't put the responsibility of bullying on your child. Usually, this happens when you try to find a reason why he/she is being bullied.

2. Try not to take it personally

Were you bullied when you were young? It's easy to take the situation personally and handle it as if it were your problem alone. Parents who were bullied as kids find themselves overwhelmed by painful memories because of their own experiences. Instead, remain neutral and use the advice you received from others that proved most helpful. Avoid what was unsupportive because it's likely not to be helpful even now.

3. Take action quickly

Bullying doesn't start with hitting and locking kids in lockers. In most cases, a bully will start with teasing and name-calling before they progress to more adverse forms. Taking action quickly ensures the situation does not escalate to these heights. You should never wait for the situation to pass on its own. If your child does not feel safe at school, take the necessary action and talk to school personnel about it. The sooner a bully is stopped the better for your child, and frankly for the bully as well.

4. Talk to the school personnel concerned

It's the school's responsibility to stop bullying, and with the rising cases of suicide and school shootings, they do take it seriously. Find a trusted teacher your child is comfortable with or talk to the school's guidance counselor. Bring notes about where the bullying took place, the form it took, and who was involved. The more information you have the better.

Emphasize that you want your child to feel safe at school, and that you are willing to work with the school to make this happen. Talk about the plan the school is willing to take and who they are willing to collaborate with to make sure your child is safe. For instance, a simple act like retreating to the guidance counselor's office to a break can give your child confidence and help them regain some control over the situation. This gives them hope that things will work out.

5. Encourage your child to stick with a friend

Having a friend during lunch, while walking home or during the bus ride is always a good idea. Bullies find it difficult to attack a 'herd' and prefer to target kids when they are alone. If friends are an issues, drive your child to and from school. Also, ask the school if they have a mentor who can watch out for him during the day.

6. Teach your child how to overcome the impact

Bullying can take a toll on your child and really put them down. Teach your kid skills and positive attitudes that can help them overcome the impact. Some parents find Tae Kwon Do and self-defense classes helpful. Boosting your child's self-confidence is vital in overcoming the effects bullying had on them.

Other problems that kids face

Unsupportive parents

Our parenting styles can be a problem for our kids. High expectations, harsh punishments, low response, and cold nurturing are characteristics of an authoritarian parent. An authoritarian expects the child to follow harsh rules while punishing any wrongdoings and giving no praise for any commendable actions.

A strict parent expects no questions and has no patience in dealing with a child. He uses shame to force the child to act expectedly. As a result, the child is obedient and usually an achiever but also shy. The kid might have issues with self-control, struggles in social situations, and often has low self-esteem.

Neglectful parents, on the other hand, could not care what happens to their kids. They are never available for their kids, either emotionally or physically. Kids from such homes often suffer from low-self esteem and engage in sex and drug use earlier than their peers. Helicopter parents, on the other hand, will hover over their kids every move and try to plan their lives for them. This usually doesn't sit well with kids because their autonomy is stifled and they have no control over their lives.

Behavioral and emotional disorder

All children tend to be naughty sometimes. For them, it's fun being naughty, even for a little while. It's the same thing adults do when they do something bad just for the fun of it. That's why, as a parent, you need to be cautious before you label your child as having a disorder. Assess their behavior for at least six months. But if a child has a difficult time and going through challenging behavior that is not normal for his age, then it might be worth a look. There are different types of behavioral and emotional disorders, which can also be known as disruptive behavior disorders. They include:

- Oppositional Defiant Disorder (ODD)

This disorder is often defined by hostile behavior, disobedience, and being defiant. The behavior is usually directed to adults and other authority figures. It's also characterized by anger, irritable moods, argumentative, and vindictive behavior.

- Conduct Disorder (CD)

It's defined by violent and disruptive behavior. Kids are aggressive, destructive, deceitful and often violate rules. For instance, they can be cruel to animals and be violent with people around them.

- Obsessive compulsive Disorder (OCD)

It's characterized by obsessions and compulsions that take up about an hour of your child's day. Obsessions are intrusive thoughts, impulses, and compulsions that consume hours of your child's day. For instance, your child may wash their hands excessively, or spend hours washing fruits before they eat.

- Attention Deficit Hyperactivity Disorder (ADHD)

It's characterised by your kid being easily distracted, they don't appear to be listening, follow the instructions, or easily forgets about daily activities. Kids often dislike activities that need them to sit still, often lose things, and tend to daydream a lot. They also don;t pay attention to mistakes and are usually careless.

Loneliness

Strange as it may sound, children too get lonely. If you asked your child what loneliness is, they would appropriately answer that; it is being sad and alone, with no one to play with them. They understand that to get away from the loneliness they feel; they need to find a friend. With isolation comes a feeling of being unwanted, which happens to everyone including kids. Kids especially feel lonely when their friends isolate them.

Peer relationships are essential, especially to growing children, because they learn a lot through interaction. Chances are a lonely child will grow into a lonely adult with self-esteem issues. They might also suffer from heart disease, stroke, or become overweight.

Several factors contribute to the feeling of loneliness in children. It can be the divorce of parents, death of a friend, family member or pet, moving to a new neighborhood or school, rejection by age mates, and so on. Some kids are shy and lack the skills necessary to make friends. Sometimes, it's because of a behavioral disorder that makes others considered them as the odd-one-out.

In today's world, which is hugely driven by social media, children are left seeking the attention of their parents. A parent can quickly lose sight of a child playing outside because they are too engrossed in their mobile phones. Sadly some of the victims are our children. Your child cannot compete against the phone for your attention.

Drug abuse

Children are introduced to drugs at a very early age, some as early as before they are born. But a good number get into drugs as a way of dealing with childhood trauma. It is crucial to deal with the negative feelings to avoid more significant issues in the future. Failure to do so, a child can result in drug use to numb the pain or fill the void in their lives. The number of children getting addicted to drugs, and growing into adults entirely dependent on drugs is astounding.

On the other hand, some kids abuse drugs because they think it is sophisticated. When you turn on the TV, there are teenage and young adults' shows that glamorize the use of drugs. That, coupled with the need to be accepted by their peers, makes it almost impossible to stay away from this dangerous habit. The days when saying no was a sign of strength, and high self-esteem are long gone. Nowadays, a kid will be called weak for refusing to partake in the debauchery.

As a parent, it is of uttermost importance to talk to your kids about drug abuse. Do not leave them to learn through social media or TV. Engage them in age-appropriate discussions. Get to hear what they know about drugs and what their thoughts are. It might seem futile at a young age, but your labor will not be in vain.

Be involved in your child's life. That way, you can notice when they are struggling or going through something. Create an open, warm, and friendly environment where your kids feel safe to talk about issues they are going through. When a child feels that he cannot get the answers they need at home, they will seek them elsewhere and who knows what they will find.

How to build real self-esteem in your child

Throughout the book, we have looked at the causes of low self-esteem and given tips on overcoming these problems. In these last few pages, we will focus on showing you how to make this possible. Reading how you should do it is one thing, but showing you how to do it will make it easier for you and your child.

1. Be a good role model and open a dialogue

Talk to your kids not only about their attention and learning issues but also on the things you see as challenging for them. Talk about your values and strength and mention how you appreciate that you have them. For instance, if your working memory is weak, say something like, "I don't remember the items

I wrote on the shopping list. Next time I'll take a picture just in case I forget to carry the shopping list."

This teaches your child that you are human, that you too have weaknesses, but you use simple methods and strategies to strengthen them. Encourage your child to come up with their own techniques and strategies to overcome their weaknesses. For instance, show them how merely pronouncing the words a little different can help them learn to spell, or how organizing your books in colors can help make homework fun.

2. Provide Clear feedback, but don't be critical

Sometimes it is hard to communicate to children on the things they have to improve on. However, addressing such topics can help your child's self-esteem development. The main point is to talk about their challenges in a motivational way to help them improve and not make them feel inadequate.

Working hard to achieve a goal leads to developing positive self-esteem. So give your child a particular purpose they can work toward, rather than criticize them. For example, instead of saying, "why are your clothes always in a mess?" You can say, "Your clothes are scattered all over the house. You can get back to your toys after you pick them up and keep them in your wardrobe."

If they have trouble spelling words, encourage them to read a simple book, and spell all the words correctly in that book. By the time they are done with three books, their efforts will have paid off, and their spelling will be much better. Help them read and listen to their spell. Praise their effort and be patient when they can't seem to get a particular word right.

3. Help in nurturing a growth mindset

Help your child to reframe negative statements and thoughts. Children with a growth mindset are confident that they can improve their abilities over time. However, children with a fixed mindset believe their abilities can't change and are set no matter how much they try. For instance, your child may say, "I have dyslexia, so I can't read this because it is too hard." You may respond by saying, "Yes, the reading may be hard for you; for this reason, you may not be able to read the book yet, but we can formulate a plan to help you read it better."

Kids need to learn how to take initiative and solve problems they face, and the first step is always through your encouragement. If you help them do it, they will have the courage to face challenges by themselves. Tori's son was fond of complaining about how bored he was in the afternoon. When Tori noticed how much he loved to paint and color, she started to commend his effort and get interested in what he was doing. When he would come complaining about being bored, Tori would tell him to figure something out. He was creative, and she was sure he could come up with something to keep himself busy while she worked.

Within a few weeks, Tori had a wall full of painted pictures, improvised toys, and other crafts that her son worked on to keep himself busy. After joining an art class, which was a way of keeping busy, has turned into a passion. Her son now is a teen and sells his paintings online to earn his allowance.

4. Teach your child that making mistakes is a learning experience

Part of possessing a growth mindset is knowing that making mistakes is learning opportunities. When your child understands that failing is ok, and there is a solution to errors, it can help to build their self-esteem. Help your child to understand the "next time you will" in his or her mistakes. You may say, "yes, you poured the juice. Next time you are pouring the juice, hold the glass over the sink."

Another excellent way to show that mistakes are a learning process is to apologize to your kids when you wrong them. Promise them that the error will never happen again and keep your word. Also, look for opportunities to openly admit you are wrong and do whatever you can to make things better.

As mentioned, kids learn through modeling. If you see your struggle to make things right, they too will follow suit.

5. Praise your child's efforts and approach not only the result

As much as praising your child is important, it matters how you do it. Instead of looking at the result, praise your child on every step he or she took along the way. By appreciating the child's approach, they enjoy tackling the challenges. You help them understand that they can overcome obstacles. Honest specific praise is vital in building positive self-esteem.

For instance, you can find ways of praising your child when they work hard on their school projects or home projects. You may say, "I see how hard you work when practicing that song on the piano. I know it was not easy, but it was a good idea asking the piano teacher some questions and for advice."

6. Encourage extracurricular mentors or interests

Look for an extracurricular activity that your child is good at and enjoys. This can help your child to discover his or her strengths as well as make academics less of a struggle. In case your child likes to sing, you can find a choir for them to join. Or if they are interested in sports, discuss how to sign up for a softball league or local soccer team.

However, if your child is not interested in any extracurricular activity, consider looking for a mentor in other interests they may have. Connecting your child with someone who is ahead of them can build and inspire confidence in your kid.

7. Point out successful people with attention and learning issues

Knowing that there are successful role models, such as celebrities, entrepreneurs, and athletes with attention and learning problems who faced the same challenges is a good source of inspiration. For instance, actor Daniel Radcliffe said that the stunt work he did for Harry Potter movies gave him help to overcome the struggles he has with dyspraxia. Lisa Nichols has dyslexia, but she has written some of the best-sellers today.

8. Encourage your child to pursue their interests.

A sure way to boost self-esteem in children is by encouraging them to do the tasks they are interested in, then see to it they do it to completion, no matter what the task is. It could be beating video games or swimming laps. The point is that they stick to what they start, for them to get a feeling of accomplishment. Help them celebrate every new achievement. It teaches your child to appreciate the effort they put into making it happen and also shows them that you can blow your own trumpet. Feel good about your accomplishment, whether you have one cheerleader, hundreds, or none.

9. Love your child

This may seem obvious, but it is the most valuable thing you can offer to your child. It doesn't matter if you do it imperfectly, who doesn't? Always pour out a lot of love. Your child desires to feel loved and accepted, starting with the family, extending to schoolmates, friends, the community, and even sports teams. If you ignore, yell or make any other parenting mistakes, see to it that you hug your child and say you are sorry and assure him or her that you love them. Unconditional love creates a strong foundation for self-esteem.

10. Model positive self-talk and self-love

Before teaching your children to love themselves, you must start by loving you. Model this by praising and rewarding yourself whenever you do well. Whether you get promoted at work, run a marathon, or throw a successful party, always celebrate your success together with your children.

Talk about the efforts, skills, and talents required for you to get those accomplishments. At the same time, remind your child of the skills she or he has and how they can use and develop them. Also, model positive body image by openly saying you love how you look or love your smiles and curvy shape.

11. Teach resilience

No one succeeds all the time. There will be failures and setbacks, pain, and criticism. Use such handles as learning encounters instead of dwelling on these events as disappointments or failures. The old sayings, try, try, and try again, has virtue, especially when teaching your child not to give up.

However, it is crucial to validate your 'skid's feelings instead of saying," Oh, cheer up," or "you should not feel so bad." This helps kids feel comfortable sharing their feelings as well as trusting them. They learn that a setback is a part of life that can be managed.

If your child doesn't perform well in a test, don't show him or her pity or tell them that they will never be good at reading. Instead, talk about the steps they can take to perform better next time. When they succeed, they will feel proud of their accomplishments, which will boost their self-esteem.

12. Instill adventure and independence

Children with high self-esteem are always ready to try new stuff without fearing failure. With younger kids, you will have to supervise them from the sidelines. You can set up situations where they can do things by themselves but make sure it is a safe situation; however, give them some space.

For instance, you can demonstrate how a sandwich is made then allow them to try it alone, without intervening or hovering. Encourage exploration, whether it is outings and day trips, new hobbies, or trips and vacations with schoolmates or teammates. This will enlarge your child's horizons as well as build their self-esteem and confidence in their ability to manage new situations.

13. Set rules as well as be consistent

Children feel confident when they are aware of what to expect and who is in charge. Although your child may feel your rules are too strict, he or she will feel confident in what they can or can't do when you have set the standards and enforce them consistently. Every household has different rules; however, they change over time, depending on the age of your child.

Whatever the rules of your household are, be specific on what's important in your family. Following and learning rules give the children a great sense of confidence and security. And as your child grows older, he or she may have extra input on responsibilities and rules. However, always remember that you are in control and you are their parent, not their best friend.

14. Coach relationship skills

Having confidence in relationships is vital to your kid's self-esteem. A loving parent-child relationship is the first relationship our child forms. It's thus, the most important. But as the social circles of your child begin to expand, you have to show him or her how their actions can affect others, and help them to learn how to maintain their self-esteem when other people's actions affect them.

As a parent, it is not your place to "mend" every situation, instead teach your child the kindness, compassion, self-assertiveness to manage the highs and lows of relationships.

Other ways to build confidence

1. Give your child choices

Giving your child choices within a reasonable preselected set of options makes them feel empowered. For instance, you can ask your child to choose between pancakes or eggs for breakfast. Learning how to make choices at a young age her for more complicated decisions she is bound to face when she grows up.

2. Don't do everything they need

Be patient and allow them to do things by themselves. For instance, it may be easier and faster to dress up your preschooler. However, allowing him or her to do it helps them learn new skills. The more they meet new challenges, the more confident and competent they feel.

3. Let them know no one is perfect

Explain to your child no one expects them to be perfect. How you react to your kid's disappointments and mistakes colors how they feel and their likelihood of sharing their frustrations and errors with you.

4. Don't offer or gush insincere praise

Children are masters at noticing baseless compliments or insincere praise. Praise your kid often, but give specific compliments so that your words don't sound hollow. For example, rather than responding to your child's drawing with," wow, that is great. You are the best artist all over the world". Try putting it like this, "I like how you have drawn the whole family. You also included details like daddy's beard."

5. Don't compare your children

Instead of comparing your children, appreciate each one's unique gifts and individuality.

6. Don't use sarcasm when making a point or call your children names

Never overlook your child's feelings; don't say anything that you might regret in anger. And always keep in mind; you can hate the child's actions without hating the child. Make sure you illustrate to your child the difference.

7. Spend quality time with your kids

Whether it is going for a bike ride or grabbing a bite, always try to schedule special time for your kids. If you have more than one, schedule special time for each and a time where all of you can be together. This is an excellent opportunity to strengthen the bond you share and talk about what is on your child's mind.

Our kids are growing up in tougher times. Teen suicide rate is soaring. One out of every three children complains of bullying. Kids are under immense pressure to perform academically. With all these stressors, it's vital to help your child maintain a high sense of self and build confidence and self-worth.

Conclusion

Every child is born with high self-esteem, but socialization changes how they view the world, their role in it, and how they feel about themselves. It's our job to guide them, so they find their way, learn to accept their faults, and celebrate their victories. Modeling high self-esteem is the best way to teach our kids.

When you are not sure of what to do, don't be afraid to tell them about it. When kids witness your confusion, they learn that even mom and dad are human beings, bound to make mistakes. Also, remember to tell your little ones that you won't stop until you find the solution. Modeling that even when things get harder, you must hold your head high, do your best, look for a solution, and trust your gut.

Outside society often brings us down, and our kids are not an exception. If your child comes to you with a problem they are facing, either at school or with their friends, be ready to lend them a listening ear, and paraphrase their words to what they really mean. Active listening will encourage them to share their problems, and help them know they have someone they can always count on, no matter what. The support we offer, the connection we make, and the words we tell our kids all join together in shaping who they believe themselves to be.

Don't hesitate to ask for help when you or your child needs it. You don't have to keep it together, even when everything seems to be crumbling around you. The best you can do is show your kids that even parents need help sometimes, and there is nothing wrong with asking someone to assist you. There is no shame in it. This too builds their confidence.

Parenting does not come with a manual, and you are likely to find yourself questioning your decisions. But, don't be discouraged, every parent goes through that sometimes. The most important thing you need to remember is that if you keep learning and doing what you know is best for your kids, you are already doing a great job. Your relationship with your child is the most important relationship they will ever form. It will shape every area of their life, and their internal blueprint will be created around the beliefs you help them build. Wake up every morning and strive to make the relationship good for them, and yourself.